THE PERFECT
PROJECT MANAGER

THE PERFECT PROJECT MANAGER

Peter Bartram

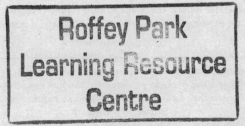

RANDOM HOUSE
BUSINESS BOOKS

First published in 1999 by Random House Business Books,
Random House, 20 Vauxhall Bridge Road, London SW1V 2SA

Random House Australia (Pty) Limited
20 Alfred Street, Milsons Point,
Sydney, New South Wales 2061, Australia

Random House New Zealand Limited
18 Poland Road, Glenfield,
Auckland 10, New Zealand

Random House South Africa (Pty) Limited
Endulini, 5a Jubilee Road, Parktown 2193, South Africa

The Random House Group Limited Reg. No. 954009

Papers used by The Random House Group Limited
are natural, recyclable products made from wood grown in
sustainable forests. The manufacturing processes conform to
the environmental regulations of the country of origin.

ISBN 0 09 940506 7

Companies, institutions and other organizations wishing to make
bulk purchases of books published by Random House should
contact their local bookstore or Random House direct:
Special Sales Director
Random House, 20 Vauxhall Bridge Road, London SW1V 2SA
Tel 0171 840 8470   Fax 0171 828 6681

www.randomhouse.co.uk
businessbooks@randomhouse.co.uk

Typeset in Sabon by MATS, Southend-on-Sea, Essex
Printed and bound in the United Kingdom by
Bookmarque Ltd, Croydon, Surrey

Contents

CHAPTER 1

Making it happen

ACCEPTING A NEW CHALLENGE

'We were wondering whether you would be able to . . .'

These words – or some very much like them – signal that you are about to be asked to take on a new project. You may hear those words at your place of work. Perhaps you are being asked to organize the company's annual sales conference, prepare the launch programme for a new product or plan the move to new offices.

Or, perhaps, you may hear those words away from the conventional work place in the fast-growing world of voluntary work. Perhaps you are a member of a parent-teacher association and are being asked to organize the school fête. Or you're tasked by a fund-raising organization with setting up a charity shop. Or you're invited to organize the annual Christmas lunch and entertainment for a senior citizens' club.

In whatever sphere, those words could signal a new challenge. You are being asked to do something that you've never done before. You are entering new and uncharted territory, and perhaps you do so with a mix of feelings. On the one hand, you're excited by the fact that other people believe you are the right person to head this important project. You're pleased that your talents are being recognized and that you're getting an opportunity to demonstrate your true worth. On the other hand, perhaps you have a secret fear – can I really do this? You're uncertain whether you can rise to the occasion and worry whether you have all the skills needed to make a success of the project.

If so, this book is for you. It sets out to show how to assemble the people and resources you need and manage the tasks you must complete to carry out an effective project. It shows how to be a perfect project manager – even if you're asked to do something you've never done before. Let's start by posing three fundamental questions.

- First: *what do we mean by a 'project'?*

A project is a self-contained piece of work with a definite beginning and a definite end. Every project starts with 'aims' or 'objectives' – what you're setting out to achieve – and ends with 'outcomes' or 'deliverables', which can best be described as what you produce if you successfully complete the project. Generally, a project has clear boundaries – which define the scope of the work – and a timetable, which sets out the period during which the work will take place. However, as we shall see, the boundaries and timetable are not always as clear as they might be.

Of course, projects come in all sizes. There are giant projects such as building the Channel Tunnel or designing and building a new jet aircraft. Such projects take years and absorb billions of pounds. There are plenty of other very large projects in areas as diverse as construction, engineering, pharmaceuticals, information technology and financial services. They may take months and carry million- or multi-million-pound price tags. Such projects will invariably be run by teams that include professional project managers using a range of planning, statistical and other specialist project management techniques. These projects do not concern us greatly in this book.

Instead, we focus on a range of small and medium-sized projects which, although they are run in a professional manner, are not managed by full-time specially trained project management professionals. It is just these kinds of projects that are likely to be headed by people who have no or little previous experience of taking on such tasks.

At the other end of the spectrum are small one-off jobs which, though they have a beginning and an end, do not warrant being described as a 'project'. Usually, these are small self-contained jobs that are carried out by one or two people. Although the jobs might need some planning, this takes place informally and the task is generally completed in a short time. We need to distinguish between these one-off tasks and a 'project' as we describe it in this book. For example, shifting two managers between different offices is a task, moving the whole company to new offices is a project. Placing an advertisement in the local newspaper is a task, developing and implementing a full-scale advertising campaign is a project.

So, the kinds of projects we'll be talking about in this book are those that fall between a small task and a large project staffed with project management professionals.

- Second: *why might you be asked to take on more projects?*

Of course, everybody's own circumstances are

completely different, but there are a few reasons why more people are going to be asked to carry out more of the small to medium-sized projects we are talking about in this book.

The first reason is to do with the changing nature of work. The old idea of a 'job for life' is gradually disappearing in all but a few industries and professions. Even in those where it seems to be assured, the nature of work changes more rapidly than it ever has before. Both these trends mean more people will find themselves working in project-based environments where they will be asked to undertake a specific task with a group of other people, some of whom they may previously never have met.

This is tied in with another key business trend. Companies are increasingly concerned to measure their performance on the basis of their 'outputs' – what's actually produced – rather than their 'inputs', such as the amount of money invested. In other words, they are less concerned with the number of hours somebody spends sitting at a desk or working a lathe, than with what's achieved as the result of those activities. This means people are given more freedom about the way they organize their work – 'empowerment' is the management term – and more work is organized around projects designed to achieve specific objectives.

Finally, one of the fastest areas of growth in work is voluntary work. Because more people retire earlier or work more flexible hours, they can take on voluntary tasks. There is no shortage of voluntary work to do. Again, much, but not all, voluntary work is project based – for example, organizing a fund-raising ball, opening a charity shop or holding a flag day. So, for all these reasons, there is more project work to do. Which means that it's more likely you'll be called in to work on a project – even lead a project. Which brings us to our final question.

- Third: *why should you accept the challenge of project work?*

Part of the answer is that more work will be project work anyway, but that's a rather negative answer. There's a more positive and challenging answer: that taking on project work, especially leading a project, stretches your working experience, enables you to learn new skills, and develops your leadership abilities.

On one level, doing all those things increases your value to the company or organization you work for. It's a way of expanding your career horizons, taking charge of your working life and moving towards the kind of future you've always hoped for yourself. It's a way of getting you out of a working rut by presenting you with new challenges, and it's a way of showing others – perhaps your bosses – just what you're capable of.

However, there's more to it than that. If you accept the challenge of a project in the right spirit – determined to succeed – you'll find the work immensely satisfying. At the outset, the task may seem challenging, even daunting. You may have some doubts about whether you've the ability to achieve it (you must be sure in your own mind that it *is* achievable), but as you tackle the tasks with your new-found colleagues, you will discover things about yourself that you never realized were there – new skills that lay dormant. When the project is finished you will have achieved more than meeting the original objectives. You will have expanded your own career or life-style horizons. It will be as though you are standing on top of a new and higher mountain, seeing far into a country that you've never previously glimpsed, and realizing that you can travel further than you ever previously imagined.

MOVERS AND SHAKERS

Before you embark on your first job as a perfect project manager, what special skills and training will you require? Probably none. In the terms in which we are defining projects in this book, you will not be called on to dip into wells of specialist knowledge. (There are plenty of projects that call for specialists – in engineering or construction, for example – but that's a different world.) In your projects, you will often need to access specialist knowledge, but that will be available from professionals and specialists and seeking it out and using the results will be one of the skills you will exercise as a project manager. (We'll look at this in more detail in chapter 2.)

Rather than looking at what you know or what you've done in the past, you need to think about five key qualities that will make you one of the movers and shakers that become perfect project managers. So what are these qualities?

1. You will be adaptable
2. You will be practical
3. You will be a creative thinker
4. You will be willing to learn
5. You will be a team worker

Let's look at these qualities in more detail:

1. *You will be adaptable*
That means you're willing to change – not reluctantly, but enthusiastically. Change is the one great certainty in

our lives. Indeed, much of modern management thought centres around how to manage continuous and profound change in large organizations. People who are resistant to change, who view any alteration in their working lives or environment with suspicion, are unlikely to make effective project managers simply because any project is, almost by definition, about creating some kind of change.

At the personal level, welcoming change is often about feeling comfortable with the new working practices, technologies and methods that you encounter in your working life. One of the greatest of these is information technology, which is, itself, changing all the time. As a rough benchmark, you often find that people who are willing to embrace change at a broader level are enthusiastic early adopters of IT. They spot the potential of computers to help them with their work.

There is also a strong link between being receptive to change and being non-judgemental about how other people organize their working lives – there is more than one way to achieve a given objective. It's important to realize that the way you choose might not necessarily be the most effective approach for somebody else. So the perfect project manager is always receptive to the new ideas that other people have to offer.

2. *You will be practical*

The kind of practical ability you need to be the perfect project manager owes little to everyday skills such as changing a plug or tuning a car engine. Critically, it is to do with the way you think. You need to be a 'whole-task thinker'. When faced with a series of objectives which your project has to achieve, you must be able not only to see the wood for the trees but also to see how the different trees in the wood inter-relate to one another.

Whole-task thinkers are able to perform a number of critical functions when they approach a problem. They are great at gathering information about the problem – particularly the kind of information that throws light on how one part of the problem is related to another part. They either have an intuitive sense for the logical connections between different actions, or they can train their mind to work out what those logical connections are. For example, they can see that it's impossible to perform one task before another is completed.

They tend to be very good at applying and balancing the resources available between the various tasks that must be finished. They're also good at making sure that the quality of performance of each of the tasks is maintained so that the whole project works and doesn't have areas that let it down – like a new car with an annoying rattle.

The theme of whole-task thinking will run through some subsequent chapters, especially when we consider choosing the team (chapter 2), deciding a timetable (chapter 3) and assembling the resources (chapter 4).

3. *You will be a creative thinker*
This quality is allied to whole-task thinking, but provides an additional dimension. Depending on your project, you may need to think of alternative ways to achieve your objectives. This is especially true when there are constraints of either time or resources on your project. If you've only a limited time to complete the task, or if you've not been granted as large a budget as you would have liked, you will need to think of alternative ways to provide the project 'deliverables'.

There is one very important way in which whole-task thinking helps the creative thinker. If you can see the whole landscape of a task mapped out in your mind, you can tell more easily which are the important parts of it and what the critical relationships are. It's then easier to focus on the priorities and test quicker or more cost-effective strategies for accomplishing your project.

4. *You will be willing to learn*

We've already mentioned that when you take on a project, it may well be something that you've never done before. Of course, you will have to learn, and no doubt you will be eager to master the key elements of the new topic with which you're grappling.

However, being truly willing to learn goes beyond a willingness to learn about things you don't know about. It includes a willingness to challenge the way you do things currently – perhaps some of your most cherished working methods – and reappraise them critically in the light of new knowledge.

Business gurus often talk about the 'learning organization' as though organizations themselves have a brain. In fact, in as much as an organizational brain does exist, it is split between all of its members. Their willingness to learn determines whether or not the organization as a whole will learn. A willingness to learn is important for any member of a project team. It is especially important for the project manager who may need to inculcate a 'learning culture' – a willingness to accept new ideas and methods – among team members who are less receptive to change than others.

5. *You will be a team worker*

Except in the smallest of projects – and we've already suggested they should be regarded as 'tasks' rather than projects – you will be working with other people. It won't be possible to complete the project to the highest possible standard unless people can work effectively as a team.

There is an important misunderstanding about team-work. It does not mean always agreeing with everything fellow team members say and never having an argument. A team in which nobody ever challenges or questions is not a team but a chain gang. What it does mean is respecting the other members of the team for the unique contribution which they bring. It means listening to their ideas with an open mind – not necessarily agreeing – and dealing with them in a frank but friendly way.

In fact, in the most effective project teams, mini debates and discussions will be taking place practically all of the time, either between some or all of the members, on the best way to complete different parts of the project. Team members will find these debates exhilarating rather than wearing, and the key role of the project leader is to develop the kind of culture in which this productive atmosphere of friendly creative tension can enhance the achievement of the project.

THE BUCK STOPS HERE

Throughout what we've been saying, we've mentioned two different ways in which you could be working in a project – as a member of the project team or as its manager. Obviously, this axiom – the buck stops here – applies chiefly to the managers, although it does no harm to have it slumbering just below the surface in other team members, project managers of the future.

In one sense, an ability to lead encompasses all the five qualities we have just discussed, but there's an extra dimension to it. It's the manager's job to provide the 'vision'. This is a rather grand way of saying that it's the manager's job to set out what the project is seeking to achieve in a way that inspires and motivates other members of the team. It's often this ability to provide a vision – what former US president George Bush once dismissively called 'the vision thing' – that makes a project team put in that extra effort which leads to really spectacular success.

Apart from the vision thing, if you're the project manager, you will have a number of important practical tasks which we'll be looking at in more detail in later chapters, so we'll just mention them here.

- As project manager, it's your task to select team members and take overall responsibility for the project team's work. (You may have situations in which unwanted project members are foisted on you and we'll deal with that in the next chapter.)

- It's your task to take the project objectives and translate them into a series of clearly defined activities that are needed to reach the objectives. In completing these activities, you'll need to manage both change and risk. You'll need to negotiate with the 'project sponsor' – the person or people for whom you're delivering the project – and other third parties who may be playing a part in completing your various activities.

- You will have the important task of defining the resources needed – unless you're working within resources that are already defined for you – and ensuring that all expenditure is properly accounted for. More than that, it will be your responsibility to make sure that your budget is most effectively spent. You will need to sort out problems that may, and almost certainly will, occur as the project progresses.

If you've never been a project manager before, that may sound like a pretty daunting agenda. And it is. We'll be looking at each of the elements in it in more detail later in the book.

There is one more task on your manager's agenda – to accept responsibility for bringing the project home on time and within budget while, simultaneously, achieving the objectives set. This is not a responsibility you can slough off on to other people. Nor will other people let you. If anything goes wrong or if you fail to bring the project home, the project's sponsor will blame you and only you. It's a simple case of: the buck stops here.

MEET THE PROJECT MANAGERS

Throughout the book, we'll be meeting three people who have completed three very different kinds of projects. Although seemingly there may not be much similarity between their projects and the one you are leading, it is surprising how the same kinds of problems crop up in very different projects.

Suzanne is the office manager for a London-based public relations company. When she took the job, she thought her responsibilities would be limited to managing the existing office and its facilities for the fast-growing agency. However, the agency was growing faster than she thought and within three months of joining, the managing director handed Suzanne her toughest assignment yet – finding new offices and organizing the move.

Tony was a high-flying salesman for a computer peripherals company. He'd imagined that he'd spend his career in the free-rolling life that a successful salesperson in the IT industry leads. Then his MD announced that the company was buying the network products division of a rival but failing company, and offered Tony the chance to be its sales director – providing he could complete the division's successful integration into the company and its relaunch. For Tony, the opportunity was as great as it was unexpected – but it called for skills he'd never previously exercised.

Margaret serves as the secretary, and only member of staff, for a small parish council in the West Country. When she took the part-time job, it seemed a simple clerical function of handling routine paperwork and servicing monthly parish council meetings. Then the council decided to sell its existing parish hall and ground to a developer and use the funds to build an improved hall in a different part of the village. Suddenly, Margaret found herself as project manager for a planning and construction project she'd never imagined.

We'll be discovering in later chapters how Suzanne, Tony and Margaret coped with some of the problems they encountered, and seeing how the lessons they learned can be of use to you too.

CHAPTER TWO

Choosing the team

IDENTIFYING SKILLS

Whatever your project, you will need a range of skills to complete it. It will be important that some of those skills should reside within the project team, while some of them can be provided by third parties. (We look at the role of third-party suppliers in chapter 4.) How do you decide which skills should be inside the team, and which brought in from outsiders? The starting point for finding an answer to this important question is to understand that there are three main kinds of skills that you need to complete the perfect project:

1. Functional skills
2. Management skills
3. Inter-personal skills

1. *Functional skills*
These are the kind of skills that people acquire either from study or, more usefully, from the experience of doing a particular kind of work over a period of time. For example, functional skills include those needed to prepare accounts, design a building, build a database or

interpret new legislation. Of course, there are thousands of other examples.

Depending on the nature of your project, you may need some of these functional skills inside the team – but which? The key question you should ask yourself is: which of these skills are essential to carrying out the project? Draw up a list of the specialist skills you are likely to need to complete the project, but think deeply about them. Have you really got to the root of what's important?

To illustrate this point, let's consider Margaret's problem. (Remember, she is the parish secretary tasked with organizing the new parish hall project.) When she started thinking about this, it seemed natural that an architect should be a member of the project team. After all, designing and building the new parish hall was at the heart of the project. Then she thought about it again. What was really important was ensuring that the new parish hall met the needs of the village – not the physical work of designing and building it. She needed to make sure the project team understood that, rather than the functional skills of designing and building. Of course, the architect attended many of Margaret's project team meetings, but he was never a full member of the team. The lesson here: think beyond the obvious to what really matters, and then make sure that those skills are represented on the project team.

2. Management skills

These skills are harder to define than functional skills but are no less important. Essentially, management skills are those used in the tasks of organizing and directing both the human and physical resources that are needed in order to meet your project objectives. Management involves skills such as planning, coordinating, control and motivation.

As project leader, you will certainly need to exercise all four of these skills yourself during the lifetime of the project. However, depending on your project, you may also want to include on your team other people with specialized management skills. Ask yourself which management skills will be especially important to make your project a success. Decide where your own skills may be deficient and try to find somebody who could help to beef up that particular area.

Consider the case of Tony who's been asked to integrate a new acquisition into his company. One of his tasks was to produce a business plan for the new division, linking the plan to the strategy of the company as a whole. Although he was familiar with the concept of business planning – especially in the way in which business plans are translated into sales targets – he had never produced a business plan himself. So, he co-opted on to his project team, in a part-time capacity, the company's financial director. The FD provided an indefinable quality often valuable in many projects – 'wisdom' – which helped Tony's project through the subtleties and, especially, the pitfalls of business planning.

There is often something very deceptive about people with the best management skills – they don't seem to be doing anything. They don't rush about solving crises, panic if things go wrong or spend frantic hours struggling with mountains of paperwork. In fact, their skill lies in that most elusive of all management qualities – the ability to look ahead and anticipate problems before they arise. If you have this ability yourself, your project team is off to a flying start. If not, finding somebody with that skill will strengthen your team immeasurably.

3. *Inter-personal skills*

It may be misleading to describe these as skills since they practically amount to personal qualities. Being a member of a project team inevitably involves working with other people. That means each team member needs the ability to be able to work effectively with these other people. There is no point having geniuses who are expert at some functional skill if they are completely unable to communicate their expertise or ideas to other members of the team, or if their way of dealing with other people is so inept or so objectionable that they rub their colleagues up the wrong way.

So this raises a critical point, one on which the success of more than a few projects has rested in the past. You must have the ability to find and bring together true team players.

FINDING TEAM PLAYERS

Just what is a 'team player'? It's possible to have endless debates about this and, finally, there is no precise answer. However, it helps to consider each person against seven key qualities:

1. Ability to listen
2. Ability to communicate
3. Honesty
4. Fairness
5. Decisiveness
6. Ability to be supportive
7. Having something to contribute

1. *Ability to listen*

Two of the important qualities all team members need are the ability to be receptive to other people's points of view and to be open to ideas. The starting point for both of these is the ability to listen. Even though this is very important, it is so rarely considered when interviewing possible candidates for a project team. Too often, the interviewers concentrate on the candidate's ability to communicate (see below) to the exclusion of other factors, but the ability to listen is an essential pre-requisite for moving forward any debate. Unless people can appreciate 'where their colleagues are coming from', there is no hope of developing the shared understanding of a problem which is, invariably, the precursor of discovering a solution.

2. *Ability to communicate*

Yes, the ability to communicate is important also, but – let's reinforce the point again – communicating effec-tively is a two-way process that also involves listening. When considering potential candidates for a project team, make sure you realize that the ability to communi-cate is not the same as the ability to talk. There are plenty of people around who are able to talk for hours on end without the ability to communicate anything useful at all. Truly effective communicators think before they talk, prioritize the information they need to provide, and give the information in a succinct way which focuses on help-ing the team to find a solution to the problem at hand.

It's worth adding that there are two kinds of communication skills you will need in your project team. The first is the ability to communicate effectively in meetings, informally with other members of the team, and with third-party suppliers. The second is the ability to write documents effectively. Not all members of your team may need to produce written material, but those that do must have this skill. Chapter 5 looks in more detail at reports and reporting.

3. *Honesty*

When we speak of honesty in connection with managing a project we are not talking about stealing a few pencils or fiddling the travelling expenses – although plainly somebody with a propensity for these kinds of activity would hardly be an ideal team member. Rather, we are thinking in terms of the personal integrity which enables a person to be 'up front' with team colleagues without causing offence. People like this gain a reputation for being sincere about their views. They tend not to express opinions just for effect or to advance some kind of private 'political' agenda. Moreover, while they are never afraid to criticize when criticism is needed – indeed, that lies at the heart of their personal integrity – they always do so fairly.

4. *Fairness*

This quality is linked to honesty. Indeed, the 'honest' person, in the terms we have defined, is also likely to be a fair person. Why is fairness so important in members of a project team? One reason is that fairness helps to set the climate in which the work of the team takes place. If every member of the team knows that all the other members are going to decide issues on their merits – rather than for external or 'political' reasons, or as a result of horse trading – then the decision-making process becomes much easier to operate. Also, incidentally, the quality of the decisions made is likely to be much higher.

The second reason is that the project itself may involve taking decisions which are going to affect the working, or even private, lives of other people. They need to have confidence that all factors will be weighed fairly in the balance before decisions are taken which may, possibly, have a wide-ranging impact. That is particularly important when the project team takes decisions which the people affected do not like. If both the criteria and process used to take the decision were transparently fair, it will be much easier to defend that decision against criticism.

5. Decisiveness

Project teams are there to make something happen, so it doesn't help if you pack your team with indecisive wafflers who can't even decide what filling to have in their lunchtime sandwich. This does not mean that you want people who will rush to judgement on every issue that confronts them. Being decisive is not necessarily about the speed with which a decision is reached. The length of time should be appropriate to the size and impact of the decision and the amount of information to be considered before taking it. Decisiveness is about taking decisions with confidence, once all the factors have been considered, then sticking by the decision once it's been made. Essentially, it's all about finding people who have confidence in their own decisions.

6. Ability to be supportive

Teamwork, quite naturally, is all about working together. It's about achieving objectives in groups, rather than individually. That means you do not want 'loners' on the team – people who secretively keep information to themselves, or take key decisions without consulting their colleagues. More than that, you want people who are prepared to work with other people in a cooperative way, who enjoy the interchanges – yes, and sometimes the arguments – that come from working with others to achieve a common objective. One secret of this is to look for people who are not so self-centred they can only think of themselves. Happily, for the team builder, the reputations of self-centred people often precede them. If not, it may become apparent at the interview (see page 24). The leader can set the tone by being supportive and helpful to other team members, and by making it clear that all members are expected to work in a mutually helpful way.

7. *Having something to contribute*

Finally, an effective team member is somebody who, quite transparently, has something to contribute. This may seem obvious, but it is not unknown for team members to be recruited for obscure motives. It is destructive for team morale if some members feel that one or more of the others are 'not pulling their weight'. From the manager's perspective, this means you should be quite clear in your own mind why you are recruiting each member of the team. What are you expecting each member to do? How will each person help to progress the work of the team? If you can't answer those questions, you must expect other team members to be confused also about why a particular person is on the team. However, when all team members recognize the value which every other member is contributing, you create a particular kind of team magic which helps to forge the team together and create the circumstances in which you can deliver great results.

PAID STAFF VERSUS VOLUNTEERS

Projects take place in both the commercial and the voluntary sector. Indeed, as we said earlier, because of the growth of voluntary work, more and more people will find themselves working on, or even leading, voluntary sector projects. In many respects, the keys to a perfect project are the same whether it is taking place in the commercial or voluntary sector. There is, however, one important respect in which there is a difference that can have quite a significant impact on the way the project is managed. Whereas in the commercial sector project team members will invariably be paid employees, in the voluntary sector the majority will be unpaid volunteers. Why is this important? There are three key points which it's worth bearing in mind.

1. Recruitment
2. Commitment
3. Management

1. *Recruitment*
In commercial sector projects, the bulk of the members of the project team will be employees of the company although there may be one or two outsiders, for example, consultants or third-party contractors who are deeply involved in the project. In the voluntary sector, you may be recruiting a project team from the members of a society, club or charity, or more widely from among members of the community. In a voluntary project, there is a natural tendency to want to accept anybody who's prepared to give up their time. Where it's difficult to find volunteers, this may seem almost irresistible. However, the wise project leader still bears in mind the seven key team member qualities discussed earlier (pp. 17–21). It may be necessary to be a little more flexible about how these are interpreted in the voluntary sector, but you ignore them at your peril. Just because somebody is prepared to give up their time 'to help' doesn't mean they will be an asset.

2. *Commitment*

In one key respect, commitment of volunteers is different from paid employees – they can't be expected to give so much of their time. Paid employees could reasonably be expected to spend all their time on a project, if that was what they were being paid for. Not so for volunteers. From a practical point of view, this means that a project leader recruiting volunteers has another important question to consider about team members. How much time can they devote to the work? It's necessary to get answers from all team members because their time commitment will partly determine the timescale over which the project can be completed. In the case of most projects, there is probably going to be a 'time threshold' below which an individual is not going to be of much value. It's the project manager's task to decide what that threshold is, and then persuade potentially valuable team members to devote more time.

3. *Management*

Many of the core concepts of project management are the same, whether it's paid employees or volunteers working, but there's a subtle difference. The old command and control approach to management – giving people orders, then standing over them while they do the work – has largely disappeared. Today, good management is much more about motivating and persuading. That's true of the commercial environment, but it's even more important in a volunteer project. In the voluntary project, the stimulus of a pay cheque at the end of the month is conspicuously missing. However, what sometimes exists in a volunteer project, which may be less marked in the commercial sector, is the shared commitment to a set of values or beliefs which binds the team together.

INTERVIEWS AND INTERVIEWING

How much interviewing you need to do for your project depends on how many people you need on your project team – and who they are. Broadly speaking, there are three different ways in which you might want to assess candidates for the project team:

1. Informal assessment
2. Informal interview
3. Formal interview

1. *Informal assessment*

In many cases, you will have already worked with people you plan to have on the project team. You will know their strengths and their weaknesses, and you might feel it would be inappropriate to interview the individuals concerned for a place on the team. Suggesting that they 'needed' interviewing might put a strain on your existing good working relationship with them and – even if they agreed to be a member of the project team after such an 'insult' – the project would start off on the wrong foot.

In these cases, you might want to assess the potential candidates privately on the basis of what you already know about them. This does not mean you should just take it as read that the individuals concerned should be co-opted on to the team. There is a case for sitting down and mapping out the questions you would have asked them had there been a formal interview. Then you can map out what the answers would have been on the basis of what you already know. The purpose of this exercise is to provide an informal audit of the skills that the particular individuals will bring to the team. It will also help you clarify in your own mind what exactly you are expecting from each of the people concerned.

At the end of this exercise, there's no reason why you shouldn't briefly explain why you're inviting each person to be a member of the team, based on the informal assessment you've carried out: 'George, I thought you'd be a valuable member of the team because of your accountancy background and experience at negotiating with suppliers.' In this way, each person knows at the point of co-option why he or she is on the team and the special contribution that's expected.

2. *Informal interview*

This would be appropriate when you know the person but not so well as to understand fully all of his or her skills and qualities – and faults and foibles. You want to get a clearer picture before you take a decision whether to invite the person on to the team, but, at the same time, the idea of conducting a formal interview from behind a desk seems too portentous.

In this case, the best approach is to explain the background to the project and ask whether the person would be interested in being considered for the team. If so, you can then suggest that it would be useful to have an informal meeting at which you could explore the possibility. The meeting can take place in your office or, less formally, over a snack lunch. However, even though it's informal, you should take care to prepare yourself beforehand, having a clear idea in your own mind of the questions you want to ask. As the meeting is informal, it's probably best to keep papers to a minimum.

You shouldn't conduct a meeting like this as if it was a formal interview. That would give entirely the wrong impression to the person you're meeting. Besides, it might put him or her on the defensive. Instead, you should seek to hold a two-way conversation in which you find the answers to your questions while, at the same time, providing the candidate with more information about the project. At the end of the meeting, you should be clear in your mind about whether the candidate is likely to be a valuable member of your project team.

3. Formal interview

This is the appropriate action when you do not know a candidate for the project team or where there are two or more potential candidates for a similar post on the project team. In this case, you should organize the interviews in a similar way to a job interview. You should provide candidates with a written brief about the proposed project in sufficient time before the interview to enable them to formulate their own ideas about it. The briefing should include a description of the candidate's proposed role on the team and what he or she will be expected to contribute.

Candidates should submit a CV before the interview, together with a short letter setting out why they feel they are the right candidate for the post. You should consider these before the interview as they may prompt key questions. In other respects, you should conduct the interview like a job interview. For more details on how to do this, see *The Perfect Interview* by Max Eggert, another book in this series.

In assembling your team, you may want to use a combination of all the techniques described here. This was what Suzanne, the public relations company office manager, did when she assembled the project team that planned the hunt for and move to new offices. She decided she needed a small team of around four or five to guide the project, and which could be used as a sounding board for various ideas about how key aspects of the move should be organized.

She informally invited one of the senior PR consultants on to the team. His contribution was to assess the proposed new offices' suitability from the operational perspective of the PR consultants in the company. She also held informal interviews with both the company's accountant and the managing director's PA before asking the accountant to join the team.

Then she held formal interviews with two consultants from a smaller PR company which her company was acquiring. They currently worked from separate offices so she did not know them well, but the plan was to consolidate the smaller agency in the new offices. Both consultants were interested in serving on the working party, but she decided one had a much more practical grasp of the problems of maintaining 'business as usual' during the move and invited her on to the team.

CHAPTER THREE

Deciding the timetable

DELIVERING ON TIME

Why is delivering a project on time so important? Does it really matter if you're a few days late?

In fact, paying close attention to the project time-scale brings into sharp focus a number of other key issues. It forces you to concentrate on all the different activities you need to complete before the project is finished. That is a vital exercise because it is the starting point of planning and implementing the whole project. So what do you need to know before you can plan your project timetable?

1. The project statement
2. The budget

1. *The project statement*

You must have a clear idea of the scope of the project, so you almost certainly need a formal 'project statement'. This is a written document which sets out what the project should deliver, and should be provided by the person or people who commission you to carry out the project. If they haven't provided you with a formal project statement, ask for one.

This next point can't be expressed too forcibly. You should be quite certain that you understand what the project statement is asking you to do *before* you embark on the work. That may sound like something that doesn't need saying, but more than a few projects have foundered because there was an 'understanding gap' between what the project sponsor *intended* and what the project team *delivered*.

This means you need to check the project statement to be certain that it tells you everything about the project that you need to know. Ask yourself questions such as these:

- Are the project objectives clearly expressed and tightly defined?
- Are there any ambiguities about the way the objectives are expressed?
- Is it clear *why* the project sponsor wants to achieve these objectives?

If you can't answer unequivocally 'yes', 'no', 'yes' to those questions, you need to ask the project sponsor to amplify the project statement.

The project statement should make it clear what the timetable is, including both the starting date and the finishing date. We'll look at this in more detail in a moment (p. 31). It should also provide an accurate statement of the project budget. We'll look at that in chapter 4. You also need to know how much authority you have in order to achieve the project objectives. For example, can you as project leader take all the decisions yourself, or do you need to have certain decisions 'signed off' by other managers or the project sponsor? If sign-offs are involved, the project statement must define them.

Beyond this rock-bottom minimum, the project statement may need to contain other information. For example, if you are conducting the project for a third party, it would need to contain details of the terms and conditions – and, probably, the fee or charges – agreed. It may need to refer to legal and safety requirements that should be observed in meeting the project's objectives. It may define the quality standards required for the work, and it may place other constraints on the way the project is carried out. Getting all this sorted out before you even start work may seem tedious, but it is essential. It will make the project run much more smoothly and, most important of all, it will ensure that you deliver precisely what the project sponsors want in the way they want it.

2. *The budget*
There is another critical exercise you need to carry out before you start work on the project. You need to be sure you can achieve what is asked within the time and budget provided. This means doing some preliminary planning to make sure that everything is possible. It's very important that you do this work thoroughly, and that you don't skimp or skirt round key issues. It may seem the easy way out to say, 'We'll look at that later', or 'We'll cross that bridge when we come to it', but that is not planning – it's reacting. It almost certainly means that your project will become seriously derailed at the first difficulty. The perfect project manager anticipates difficulties *before* they arise and plans to deal with them.

So, to return to the original question, does it really matter whether you deliver your project on time? Most certainly it does, and for two reasons.

First, other important activities may depend on you bringing your project home on time. In Suzanne's case, the growth of her public relations agency was being held back because it didn't have large enough offices. In the case of Tony, a key sales campaign was on hold until the new division was integrated with existing activities. Put bluntly, you should make every effort to deliver on time because other people are relying on you to do so.

Second, do you want to gain a reputation as somebody who's always late? That's not a way to persuade other people to entrust you with interesting projects, or to advance your career. It's true that time pressure is something that's constantly increasing in the business world, but people who can cope with that – even thrive within that environment – are going to be among the high-flyers of tomorrow.

TECHNIQUES FOR TIMETABLING

So how should you set about timetabling your project? The timetable will act, first, as a means of testing the project's viability within the timescale and, second, as a planning and control document as the project progresses.

Just how sophisticated you need to get in timetabling your project obviously depends on its size and scope. For the very largest projects, timetabling and scheduling is virtually a project in its own right – but here we are dealing specifically with small and medium-sized projects.

What do we need to consider?

1. The work breakdown structure
2. Timetable tools

1. *The work breakdown structure*
The first step in developing a timetable for your project

is to understand in more detail the scope of the work that needs to be done, and you can do this quite simply by developing a 'work breakdown structure'. Essentially, this is a tree-structure diagram in which each box represents a specific piece of work or 'task'. The work breakdown structure not only helps you divide and sub-divide large activities into smaller tasks, but it also helps you relate the small tasks within larger activities and, ultimately, within the project as a whole. This gives you a simple map of how the different pieces of work in the project fit together.

It pays to let all the members of the team become involved in developing the work breakdown structure because some will understand the work that needs to be completed in their part of the project better than others. Besides, if all the members make a contribution to planning the project, you are involving them as a team right from the outset, and you are also less likely to overlook a key activity or task.

2. *Timetable tools*
Once you've developed an adequate work breakdown structure, you have a choice in deciding how to timetable your project. The very simplest projects might be timetabled using a large wall calendar on which you mark the start and finish dates of each of the tasks in the project. This has the merit of being simple and not taking much time to do. On more complex projects, however, it may be a little too simple to capture the full complexity of the relationships between the different tasks and the impact they could have on project progress.

For those project managers who want to move to a rather higher degree of sophistication, there are two main choices, which are not necessarily mutually exclusive: the Gannt chart and the Pert chart.

The Gannt chart is named after Henry Gannt, the early-twentieth-century American who first popularized it. A Gannt chart lets you list the target start and finish dates of each of the tasks in your project, and then define the relationships between them with arrows. One key benefit of a Gannt chart is its ability to show graphically which tasks need to be completed before other tasks can begin. Moreover, a Gannt chart is a good visual control tool. You start off with all the tasks represented as open boxes and shade them in as each task is completed. In this way, an unshaded box on any part of the chart prior to the current date stands out as a task that is running behind schedule.

You can run a Gannt chart on paper. Indeed, you can buy from a good stationer large sheets of graph paper on which you can draw your own. There are also a number of software packages that let you run a Gannt chart on your PC. The packages are comparatively inexpensive and can repay their investments – and the small amount of time needed to learn how to use them – if you have a project that's sufficiently complex to warrant it, or if you're likely to be running more projects in the future. Ask your local PC suppliers about the options.

However, once you get past approximately fifty different tasks in a project, a Gannt chart can become a little unwieldy, particularly if it's a paper Gannt chart. A PC-based chart can accommodate more, although even this starts to become cumbersome to use once the number of tasks grows towards a hundred, simply because it becomes increasingly complex to represent the linkages between all the different tasks. If this is the case you may want to consider using a Pert chart.

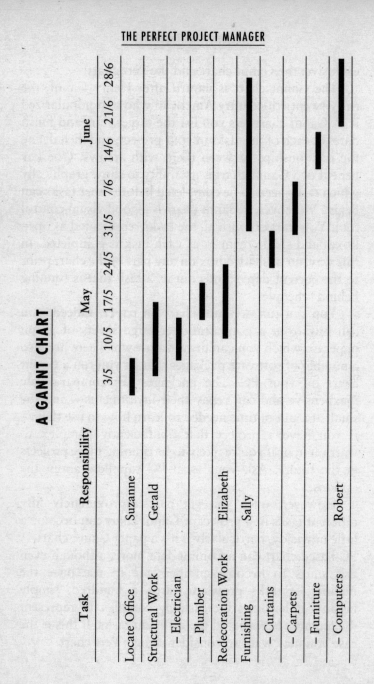

A GANNT CHART

Task	Responsibility	May				June			
		3/5	10/5	17/5	24/5	31/5	7/6	14/6	21/6	28/6
Locate Office	Suzanne								
Structural Work	Gerald								
– Electrician									
– Plumber									
Redecoration Work	Elizabeth								
Furnishing	Sally								
– Curtains									
– Carpets									
– Furniture									
– Computers	Robert								

34

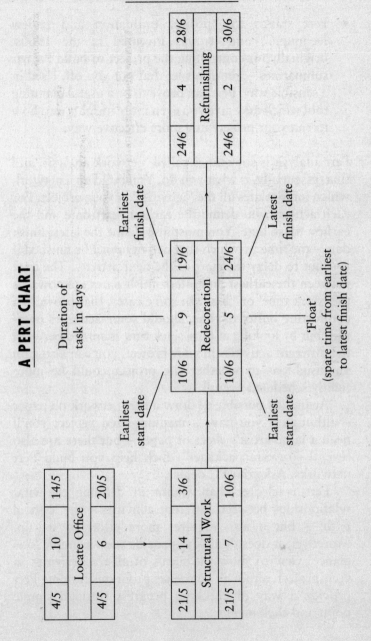

A PERT CHART

4/5	10	14/5
	Locate Office	
4/5	6	20/5

21/5	14	3/6
	Structural Work	
21/5	7	10/6

Earliest start date

Duration of task in days

Earliest finish date

10/6	9	19/6
	Redecoration	
10/6	5	24/6

Earliest start date

Latest finish date

'Float' (spare time from earliest to latest finish date)

24/6	4	28/6
	Refurnishing	
24/6	2	30/6

- Pert stands for 'project evaluation and review technique', and it was invented in the 1960s, originally for controlling the project to build Polaris submarines – but don't let that put you off. Used in a sensible way, Pert can prove to be a useful planning tool which may give you even more insights into how to run your project in a more effective way.

Pert analysis is sometimes called 'network analysis' and that, essentially, is what you do. You build up a network which inter-relates all the 'activities' in your project. For each activity you define the earliest start date and the earliest finish date. You must also define the latest finish date – the time by which that activity *must* be finished if it is not to delay the start of the next activity. The time between the earliest and latest finish dates is known as the 'slack time' or 'float'. In some cases, that provides a comforting buffer of time, should some activities over-run, but by looking at how slack time is spread between the different activities in your project, you can also gain an insight as to whether the project could be more tightly scheduled overall.

Again, it's possible to draw a Pert network on paper – although if you have a medium-sized project you'll need a large artist's sheet of paper – but there are also several software packages which help you build Pert networks. Ask your PC dealer.

Pert is clearer than Gannt in defining the vital relationships between different activities – the 'critical path' – but it also requires more effort to set up. Moreover, it doesn't always provide such a simple 'one glance' view to show the status of all the activities in your project, although computer programs running Pert provide a way of checking progress through simple point and click menus.

*

So, how should you choose which method to use? The best guidance is to choose the simplest method that will do the job. That means both the simplest technique – whether calendar, Gannt or Pert – and the simplest method of doing it, either on paper or computer. It's very important to avoid the danger of 'analysis paralysis' in which you spend so much time exploring different ways of carrying out the project that you never actually get down to the work. On the other hand, there are also very real dangers in insufficient planning. It's a question of balance. You need to judge just how much planning you need in order to develop the project timetable, and then ensure that it's adhered to as the project proceeds.

How did our three project leaders approach this issue?

Suzanne used the calendar approach. She bought a large blank planning calendar from a stationer and planned the project on it with her team members. She used pencil first, as that could easily be rubbed out and changed. Then, when everybody was happy, she converted her pencil markings using different coloured felt-tipped pens. Each team member's tasks were in a different colour so it was easy to see who had to do what – and when.

Tony used a Gannt chart running on his PC. As a computer industry professional, he already had access to suitable software. He reckoned his project, which involved integrating a new division into the company, was sufficiently complex to warrant the degree of formal planning that Gannt provided. Using the Gannt on the PC helped him to test a few what-if scenarios before the project began, thus enabling him to slice a few days off the timetable and reschedule some time-critical activities more effectively. Tony also found Gannt an effective way of monitoring progress.

Margaret faced a quandary when she started the project to relocate the parish hall. She hadn't even heard of Gannt or Pert. Happily, the construction company that was awarded the contract for building the new hall had used a PC-based version of Pert for years. One of the managers offered to help Margaret and her project team to use it to plan the whole move – of which the actual construction of the hall was just a part. It was an offer Margaret was pleased to accept. This proved highly effective as it was possible to link Margaret's Pert chart to the one used by the construction company and so monitor progress on the building of the hall alongside other activities.

PROJECT TIME TRAPS

You have your project timetable and nothing can go wrong. Of course it can! And probably will. There are plenty of specific reasons why your project timetable may get blown off course, but most of these reasons boil down to one of the ten following project time traps.

1. *Project sponsors not making up their minds*
Beware project sponsors who ask you to carry out a project, but don't seem to know quite what they want. They think they've commissioned you to start the project – but they haven't even provided the all-important project statement. They think work is already under way – you know it hasn't even started because you don't know what to do. That's why it's important for the project statement to contain a clear start date. Then everybody knows exactly when the clock on this particular project starts ticking.

2. *Project sponsors always changing their minds*

Nothing wastes time more than project sponsors constantly changing their minds (although a limited number of changes may be necessary, even desirable). It can cut away days of work, and perhaps even thousands of pounds. Again, this is a very good reason for ensuring that the project statement is clear from the outset. However, if the project sponsors do change their mind – perhaps for very good reasons – make sure the time implications of the change are clearly spelt out straight away. If the project is going to take longer, the project sponsors need to understand that it's down to them and not you.

3. *Not assembling the resources soon enough*

As we shall see in chapter 4, assembling the resources for your project is an important task. It's essential not to start this too late. For one reason or another, there may be delays in providing certain resources that you don't know about, and even when resources have been ordered for specific dates, your suppliers may let you down. With so much to do, it's very easy to order goods that are urgent and leave the acquisition of resources you won't need for next week or next month until later. That just invites hold-ups.

4. *Doing each job one at a time*

In timetabling your job, you will have discovered which jobs need to be completed before others begin. It may seem simple and tempting to carry out each job one at a time, sequentially. In fact, many of the jobs can be done in parallel and you'll save considerable amounts of time as a result. In planning, look for opportunities where activities can be run alongside one another.

5. *Not setting up the project professionally*
You certainly don't need to splash out on luxury offices and the latest state-of-the-art computers, but there is plenty to be said for making sure you have appropriate accommodation and the equipment you reasonably need before you start the project. Not having key items will slow you down and you may have to waste time later in the project in order to acquire office furniture, equipment or even extra space you should have had from the outset.

6. *Operating with too dispersed a project team*
In many cases, members of a project team will work from the same office. In other cases, project team members may work from different locations. With modern methods of electronic communication, such as e-mail and video-conferencing, that may not prove too much of a problem. However, if team members need to spend a lot of time together or hold meetings, travelling time can steal away the hours.

7. *Wasting time on meetings*
All projects need meetings, and some projects quite legitimately need a lot of meetings, but it's important to make sure that time is not wasted. So, have a proper agenda for each meeting and don't deviate from it. Keep the number of people attending a meeting to a minimum. Try to hold meetings at times that stretch the working day, for example, over breakfast or in the early evening.

8. *Spending too much time arguing about detail*
Of course, it's possible to have disputes among the project team about matters of substance. Most arguments, however, tend to flare up over details –

sometimes largely irrelevant details. It's the job of the project manager to make sure that such arguments don't get out of control and that the amount of time spent discussing an issue is proportionate to its significance.

9. *Striving for impossible perfection*
Naturally, you want your project to achieve outstanding results, but you must understand that perfection is an impossible dream. All projects take place within constraints of time and money and it's important to understand from the outset what those constraints mean for what it's possible to achieve. Then set out to achieve that as well as you can.

10. *Holding post mortems on set-backs*
All projects have their set-backs – things that go wrong or plans that don't turn out quite as was intended. It's important to learn from set-backs, but there is a danger during the project of spending too much time on detailed post mortems. What's done is done, and you need to put it right as quickly as possible to get your project to the finishing line on time. By all means, hold more detailed post mortems after the project is finished.

CHAPTER 4

Assembling the resources

LISTING WHAT YOU NEED

With your project timetable in place, you're ready to make a list of all the resources you will need as you carry out the project. There are three reasons that it is very important to be clear about what you need to complete the project even *before* you start it – and even though on a lengthy project it may seem more sensible to assemble your resources as you need them.

- First, without building up a clear resources picture, you are not able to produce a detailed project budget. Consequently, you won't know whether you can complete the project within the funds available, and as the project progresses, you won't be able to monitor expenditure against budget.

- Second, defining all the resources you need at the outset helps in the planning process. It reinforces the work you've already done on timetabling and the linkages that exist between different activities. Indeed, as you set about defining the resources, you may even discover new linkages and dependencies that you'd missed when you were mapping out your timetable.

- Finally, by defining your resources at the outset, you're in a position to start planning how to acquire everything you need. You have the time to shop around for some items to get the best prices, and you discover whether some items are hard to obtain. If they are, you have enough time to make arrangements to obtain them. It's important to remember that the cost of obtaining emergency supplies at the last minute is invariably more expensive than ordering well in advance.

WHAT RESOURCES WILL YOU NEED?

Very broadly they fall into three categories:

1. Third-party skills
2. Goods
3. Materials

although sometimes the edges between goods and materials are a bit blurred.

1. *Third-party skills*

Your project may call for some, or even significant, input from third-party consultants or professionals. It's impossible to generalize, but you might need the services of lawyers, accountants, architects, surveyors, designers, artists, photographers, writers, sign-painters, landscape gardeners, plumbers, electricians, software programmers . . . The list is almost endless. The key factor about all of them is that they *do* something rather that provide specific *goods*. As a result, the key factor you need to be concerned about is the quality of the service they provide.

2. and 3. *Goods and materials*

You may need a range of goods and materials in order to complete your project. Obviously, whatever your project needs depends entirely on what it is. It's not even sensible to try to give a list here – it could include virtually anything can think of. However, you can get an idea from some of the goods and materials each of our three project leaders needed to source. Suzanne, who organized the office move of her public relations consultancy, needed to source carpets and curtains for the new offices, some new office furniture and a multitude of other office furnishings, right down to some new indoor plants. Tony, who was integrating the division of another company into his, had to source computers and software for the new employees as well as a range of office furniture. Margaret, who was organizing the building of the new parish hall, merci-fully did not need to source all the building materials – that was down to the construction company. However, she did, as an example, need to source all the equipment for the new hall's kitchen.

A sound approach is to list the resources you need alongside the timetable for the project. Think carefully about each activity within the timetable and consider the resources – in all three categories – that you will need to complete that activity. Look for activities where you will need the same or similar resources. It may save time, and possibly money, to order them at one time.

SOURCES AND DELIVERY

It is not enough just to list the resources you need. You must also carry out two other essential tasks at this stage.

- First, you need to decide on *where* you are going to source each of the resources you need. For some resources – computers or stationery – that may not be a difficult task as there are thousands of possible suppliers. However, you still need to determine which will offer the best price and service in your own special circumstances. For other resources, it may be more difficult to find a supplier. A good starting point for this is always the most obvious – *Yellow Pages*. If this fails to produce the contacts you need, it's worth visiting a good reference library. Most contain a wide range of trade and professional directories. Some list trade associations which can provide names of possible suppliers in your area. Finally, it may be worth searching the Internet. Thousands of UK companies now have web sites – although the problem is that Internet 'search engines' will also present you with suppliers in other parts of the world, mostly the United States.

- Second, you need to determine the delivery *lead time* for each of your resources. Don't assume that just because something sounds easy to obtain, you can get it tomorrow. It may be out of stock, or there may be other delivery problems. Determining lead times is just as important when you are booking third-party skills. Tradesmen and professionals may be committed to other projects and need notice to fit your work into their schedules. The sooner you start to determine the lead times, the more likely you are to avoid unexpected hold-ups later in the project.

PREPARING A BUDGET

There are two different sets of circumstances in which you may be asked to produce a project budget. In the first, you are given a set figure which is what you have to spend, and you must achieve the project's objectives within that sum. In the second, you are tasked with producing a budget which defines what it would cost to achieve certain objectives. There are important points which flow from each of these approaches.

The fixed budget

When you have a fixed budget, it's absolutely essential at the planning stage – when you're drawing up your timetable and defining and listing the resources – to determine whether you can complete the project within the money you've been given. It can't be stressed too strongly that you need to be totally confident of completing the project within the agreed sum *before* you start on it. If you begin the project 'hoping for the best' and run out of money part of the way through, your bosses will not look kindly on your requests for more cash. Moreover, the blame will fall on you for 'poor budgeting', rather than on the project sponsor for providing an inadequate sum in the first place. If you're convinced the budget is insufficient, say so at the outset. If your project sponsor is not prepared to increase the budget, either renegotiate the scope of the project, so that it can be completed for the sum available – or walk away.

Defining the cost of a project yourself

When you are developing a budget to determine the cost of a project, you are in a rather different position. In this situation, the project sponsors are telling you they don't know how much the project will cost. The budgeting exercise is, in effect, a self-contained phase designed to determine whether the project can be carried out for a sum of money that the project sponsors can afford. In this situation, you might have more flexibility about how you structure the project and there may even be a case for offering alternatives – at different prices – in some parts of the project. In this situation, you need to have the budget you've developed approved *before* you start work on the project proper.

When you're drawing up a project budget, you must be clear which costs need to be included. This may seem straightforward but there are, in fact, a number of grey areas which can cause difficulties if they're not tackled at the outset. For example, within a company you need to determine:

- whether the salaries and National Insurance of the project team members should be included in the project budget. If some team members are working for the project on a part-time basis, do their salary costs need to be included on a *pro rata* basis?

- do general office and facility costs need to be included in the project budget? For example, should the budget make a *pro rata* allowance for the costs of rent and rates? Should items like electricity, use of computers, photocopying and so on, be included when the project team is using facilities which are already available within the company?

It's important to get clear answers to both these questions – preferably written down in the project statement – before beginning work on the budget.

Drawing up the budget

Having sorted out these important preliminary issues, you're ready to get down to the work of drawing up the budget. You've already defined the resources you require and you now need to determine the cost of those resources. This will usually involve getting written quotations from potential suppliers, although in the case of minor supplies an informal verbal estimate may be acceptable. The key point is that you should be confident that each figure that goes into your budget is accurate. It's wise to err on the side of caution when including individual figures. A single under-estimate may not be a disaster but a cumulation of under-estimates can wreck a budget.

The tools you use to prepare your budget depend on its complexity. If the budget contains only a few items, then it may be adequate to prepare it on paper, using pre-printed accountants' analysis sheets available from good stationers. If your budget is more complex, you may want to use a computerized spreadsheet or a formal budgeting system running on a PC. Whichever method you choose, you must be sure that you can easily and accurately monitor expenditure against budget as the project progresses. Ask yourself whether you will be able to do this on at least a weekly, possibly even a daily, basis with your chosen budgeting tool. If not, you've chosen the wrong tool and need something a little more sophisticated.

When it came to budgeting, Suzanne elected to keep track of the budget and costs incurred on multi-columned accountants' analysis sheets. She thought the number of different headings would make this possible. In fact, the project proved more complex than expected and the budget was more difficult to track. She managed, but it took more time than she would have liked. By contrast, both Tony and Margaret used computerized budgeting tools to track their projects. Tony, an old hand with computers, used the standard spreadsheet software already on his PC. Margaret had the help of the parish hall's main contractors who used their own budgeting software to create a budget for the overall project.

DEALING WITH THIRD-PARTY SUPPLIERS

What, exactly, are 'third-party' suppliers? The most obvious ones are those organizations, outside your own, which are supplying goods and services or special skills and expertise to help complete the project. They could be supplying any of the resources. However, in another sense, it could be sensible to regard anybody outside the immediate project team and its co-workers as a 'third-party' supplier – including other departments of your own company that are asked to perform specific tasks for the project.

The key factor about third-party suppliers is that they are not under your direct management or control, they are not within your immediate chain of command. That means you cannot manage the relationship you have with them in the same way you manage the members of the project team. Yet the work third-party suppliers do can be of considerable importance to the success of the project. So the relationships must be managed, and they must be managed effectively. A third-party supplier who fails to deliver can undermine the whole viability of your project, but they will escape the direct wrath of your project sponsor – that will fall on you.

Consider some of the third-party suppliers encountered by our three project leaders to see just how important they can be. Suzanne's whole project ultimately rested on how successfully the office removal company she employed performed its work. Suzanne wasn't looking for a team of box movers, she wanted a company that would put in that extra effort to ensure the complex move could be completed over a weekend, with the new office up and running by nine o'clock on Monday morning.

Similarly, Margaret struck lucky with the construction company that was the prime contractor on her parish hall project. The company went out of its way to use their expertise to help her plan the rest of her project.

In fact, Margaret didn't just strike lucky – her project team's choice owed more to judgement. That's a critical point with third-party suppliers. When you're choosing them, you need to pay close attention to whether or not you think you'll be able to work closely and effectively with them. Do they seem to be on the same wavelength as you? Do they look as though they'll want to be helpful? Do they sound as though they really want your business? Are they prepared to go that extra mile to ensure you get what you really want? These are questions you must ask when you're choosing the critical third-party suppliers for your project – those who can make or break it.

Getting the best from your supplier
When you're negotiating with third-party suppliers bear in mind a couple of key points:

- You are the customer so you're entitled to behave

like a customer and insist you get what you want. However, remember that how important you are as a customer will depend on the size of your business, the size of the supplier and whether or not you're likely to be a regular source of new orders to them. Other factors being equal, it's sometimes a good idea to choose suppliers of equivalent or smaller size to yourself. They'll often be hungrier for your business and more anxious to please.

- Remember that even though the supplier may be keen to win your business, it also has its own goals and objectives. If you can understand those, you're in a better position to gain more value from them. For example, your project might be giving the supplier valuable new experience, taking it into a new market or providing a reference site it can use to help win future contracts. The best kind of working relationships are those where both parties – the customer *and* the supplier – are getting more out of it than they originally imagined. So, while keeping your key project objectives 'front of mind', also look for opportunities to work cooperatively with third-party suppliers.

The contract
The relationship between your project and your third-party suppliers will generally be governed by a contract of some kind. How formal or complex that contract is depends on the size and significance of the work the supplier is doing. In the case of comparatively minor suppliers, a simple letter may be sufficient to formalize the arrangement. In the case of rather more complex relationships, a memorandum of agreement may be appropriate. The most important contracts should be based on formal documents drawn up with appropriate

legal and other (for example, technical) advice.

Whatever the contract, it should always stipulate exactly and precisely what is to be delivered or done, where it is to be delivered or done, the price (or how the price will be determined), the delivery date or dates and, in the case of the most important contracts, the penalty payments to be made by the supplier in the event of non-compliance with the contract. Whether a simple letter or a hundred-page contract, never rush it, and always give careful consideration to what you're asking for. It may be expensive to make changes later.

Keep communication channels open

When you've agreed what your third-party suppliers are going to do, don't try to micro-manage how they do it. They have their own ways of working which, if you've chosen wisely – should be effective. It's best to let them achieve your objectives in their way. However, do focus your attention on the results. It does no harm in a big job to have a series of milestones along the way, at which you either formally or informally monitor progress with your third-party supplier and satisfy yourself that you're happy with what is being done.

One final point with third-party suppliers. Make sure they have all the information they need to perform their work. One of the biggest problems in projects is lack of adequate communication, partly among members of the project team but mostly with third-party suppliers. Don't assume you've told your suppliers everything they need to know once you've signed the contracts. In any complex project, there will always be issues that need clarification or problems that need resolving. As project leader your ever-open door should welcome third-party suppliers as well as members of your team.

OVERCOMING SUPPLY PROBLEMS

No matter how carefully you choose and brief your third-party suppliers, things will sometimes go wrong. By giving proper attention to each of the following seven actions, you can reduce the chances of problems and put them right more quickly when they do occur.

1. *Check credentials of suppliers*

Wherever possible, try to get independent verification of the quality of goods or services of any of the major third-party suppliers you're planning to use. Look especially for their ability to deliver on time, within budget and to specification. Find out how they react when problems occur and something needs to be put right. Are they keen to put things right or do they point the finger of blame elsewhere? Are companies that have used them before planning to use them again? Don't forget to check on the supplier's financial stability.

2. *Allow adequate lead times*

Sometimes supply problems are self-inflicted when project managers don't allow enough time for third-party suppliers to deliver the highest quality goods or perform their best work. Find out right at the start of the project what the lead time is for each major third-party supplier to perform its functions. Then add a little bit extra on top to allow for time slippage.

3. *Define quality standards*

Make sure each third-party supplier understands, *before* you even sign the contract, the quality you require from its work. This applies whether the supplier is providing goods or specialist services. Project delays are often caused when work proves to be below the standard expected and has to be put right. Often, this delays other activities which are dependent on its adequate completion.

4. *Identify alternative or back-up suppliers*

When you are defining the resources, it is useful to identify more than one supplier for key tasks. When evaluating your first choice, keep in mind which company would be your second choice. Keep lines of communication open to it – you never know when you might need its help at short notice.

5. *Institute a problem early-warning system*

Insist that third-party suppliers give you early warning if there is likely to be any problem with them completing their task on time and within specification. An early warning system could take one of several forms – for example, a weekly or monthly check to review progress or outstanding problems. Encourage suppliers to come to you early with any potential problems and be receptive when they do so – don't develop a 'blame culture'.

6. *Take remedial action immediately*

When something starts to go wrong, move fast to put it right. Don't assume that 'it will all come right in the end'. It won't. In fact, it will probably get worse and become even more expensive and time-consuming to rectify. Consider forming a special task force to tackle any major problems that occur during the course of a project. Attach higher priority to finding solutions than apportioning blame.

7. *Stage payments to third-party suppliers*

Where third-party suppliers are performing large

contracts and require stage payments, make sure that payments are linked to reaching key milestones in their work. Ensure that stage payments are not more than proportionate to the amount of work already done. In fact, try to weight payments towards the end of the contract, and never agree to make full payment until work has been delivered and signed off as being of the required standard.

CHAPTER 5

Assigning responsibility

LINES OF RESPONSIBILITY

You've chosen the members of your project team (see chapter 2). Now you have to assign responsibility and create the right kind of structure in the team which will enable them to do their work effectively and you to manage the project properly. It's important to remember that projects, by their very nature, bring together people who've not previously worked as a team. In chapter 6, we'll be exploring some of the things you can do to make sure your team works well together. However, there's also the question of setting up a formal framework for the management of the project and assigning everybody their place in it.

In many projects, the team comes together with a great deal of excitement and enthusiasm. As everybody gets to know one another, there's a danger that some of the fundamentals of planning could be overlooked. Of course, it's very important that the team should 'bond' and develop the shared and common purpose that's so important in successful projects. It's equally important that individual members of the team should be quite clear what their own role in the project is, what they're expected to achieve and how their contribution fits into the whole.

Assigning roles

The responsibility for this lies with the project manager. Unless the manager assigns roles and sets up clear lines of responsibility nobody else will.

So what should the manager be doing at the outset? To begin with, as manager you will have chosen each member of the team – so you should have a clear idea *why* you've chosen each person. Think back to chapter 2 when we described the functional, managerial and inter-personal skills that team members could contribute. Among all your team members, you should now have a rich mix of those skills, and you should set about assigning roles to make the best possible use of them.

Every team member should have a crystal clear understanding why they are a member of the team and what they're expected to contribute. One of the problems with some projects is that roles and responsibilities are not defined tightly enough. People have a rough idea what they're supposed to be doing, but a rough idea is not good enough. Rough ideas lead to rough solutions, and your project should be all about achieving excellence.

There are two stages to tackling this problem:

- First, as project manager, you must define the roles and responsibilities of each member of the team, including yourself. Go back to the objectives as defined in your project statement in order to help you define individual roles and responsibilities. Write down the roles and responsibilities of each member of your team, setting out clearly what they're expected to do, what decisions they're permitted to take, and which other member of the team – probably yourself as manager – they report to.

- Second, you need to communicate the roles and responsibilities to each member of your team. It's useful if team members understand not only their own tasks but those of other team members. They can then see how what they have to do fits into the bigger picture. Probably the first meeting of the project team should be partly devoted to this.

The first team meeting

As project manager, you should introduce all team members to one another and explain clearly what each will be doing. Take time to discuss the roles of individual team members and be prepared to amend your original ideas. If you've chosen a good team, they will have valid ideas about how to achieve your objectives and you ought to take these on board. At the end of the meeting, everybody in the team should have a clear understanding not only of their own roles and responsibilities but of those of other team members.

After the meeting, you should make sure that you write out a final statement, including any amendments agreed at the meeting, of the roles and responsibilities of each team member. Team members should have a copy of their own role and responsibility statements, and there may be a case for handing out the statements of all members to everybody. In this statement, you may want to include a chart showing how the team is organized diagrammatically and what the different reporting lines are. On a smaller project, however, where the team consists of only a handful of members, this may seem a bit pretentious.

The role and responsibility statement

What should a role and responsibility statement contain? Much will depend on the size and complexity of the project as to how detailed it is.

- At a minimum, it should contain a clear statement of what the individual is expected to achieve, and over what timescale.

- The statement should say which decisions the team member can take and which should be referred to either the manager or the whole team.

- The statement should also make clear, if relevant, how much budget the individual has to achieve his or her objectives.

- Finally, it may be useful to include a statement of the quality standards that apply. In the largest projects, these may be international or British Standards Institution standards. In smaller and medium-sized projects, quality statements should focus more on the standard of specific outcomes that the project must deliver. In other words, the quality statement is not so much about what needs to be done as how well it must be completed.

GETTING THE BEST OUT OF PEOPLE

You need members of the project team to understand their roles and responsibilities clearly, but you don't want them to be so weighed down that they crumple under the pressure. In fact, you want to create the kind of working environment in which people can give of their best, and even find that something extra inside themselves which they didn't realize they had. Part of the secret of this is to get everybody working effectively as part of a team and we'll look at that in detail in chapter 6. How else can you get the best from your team?

The basics

At the outset, it's very important to make sure that all members of the team have what they need to accomplish their tasks effectively. For example, have they adequate office accommodation, the computer they need, access to resources such as photocopying and so on? Although these are basic questions, they can undermine both the morale and performance of team members if they are not addressed at the outset.

The working environment

With the basics in place, it's important to create a working environment in which individuals want to contribute their best – to go that extra mile – in helping to bring the project home on time and to the highest possible standards. It can't be stressed too strongly that responsibility for this rests with the project manager. As manager, you need to display certain qualities to members of your team:

- The first is a complete confidence in the value of the project. If you don't demonstrably feel that the project is worthwhile, then your team members will wonder what the purpose of their presence is. That may seem an obvious point to make but some project managers fail to communicate the excitement they feel about what they're setting out to do. In communication with team members be upbeat, not downbeat.

- The second is in being an effective mentor, especially to those team members who may initially lack confidence and need some extra encouragement. You become an effective mentor as much by the attitudes you display as by the practical help you offer. If your attitude is consistently positive and helpful – even in the face of difficulties – other members of the team will take their cue from you. The manager sets the tone for the team and if you are conveying negative signals – frustration, annoyance, unfair criticism, procrastination and so on – other members of the team will tend to follow your lead.

- As manager, it's also important for you to make space in your working schedule to spend time helping other members of the team. This doesn't mean that you should do their work for them. Rather, that you should keep a close eye on what they're doing and anticipate problems that may arise before they do. For example, if you see a team member struggling with a particular task, try to address it with him or her in a private and tactful way before the problem grows. The very fact of knowing that you're on their side in a very practical way will give team members considerable confidence to tackle tasks that may be new to them.

- Another way in which the manager can help team members is in deflecting external pressure or criticism – especially what may be 'political' pressure from other parts of the company, or unfair criticism from non-team people. This is especially true if a member of the team has a difficult task which is bound to ruffle a few feathers or even encounter outright opposition in some quarters. It's important that, as manager, you don't leave one team member to deal with this alone. Criticisms ought to be taken as of the team as a whole, and dealt with in that way.

Two of our three project managers encountered problems with their teams. Suzanne found that Jilly, one of her team members, was under pressure because she was still expected to carry out all her normal work as well as fulfilling her duties on the project team organizing the office move. Suzanne had a quiet word with Jilly's boss. The outcome: some of Jilly's normal work was taken over by other people until the office move project was complete.

Tony found that Jon, one of the members of his team, hadn't understood his brief correctly. Jon's function in the project was to make a careful point by point comparison of the acquired division's products with the products in the company's existing range. Tony found that Jon was treating this as an exercise to score the benefits of the existing products over the new division's. Tony explained that the aim was to bring together both product lines and sell the benefits of both as an integrated range. Once Jon had grasped this point, his performance on this task soared.

REPORTS AND REPORTING

Nobody likes bureaucracy and that's why it's tempting to treat reports and reporting as an unnecessary inconvenience in a project. This is particularly true where the project seems to be going well and where members of the team are getting along with one another just fine, communicating regularly and informally by word of mouth. Plainly, you do not want to become involved in writing thick reports or spending hours in time-wasting formal reporting sessions. However, there are powerful reasons why you should introduce some formal reporting procedures into your project.

Why you need reports

- *To demonstrate correct procedures.* In even the smallest and most informal of projects, you may need to demonstrate that you've taken decisions and carried out work in the proper way. For example, you may need to show that decisions have been signed off by the appropriate manager or official, that expenditure has been properly incurred and that health and safety rules and regulations have been correctly observed. Even if your project comes in on time and within budget, and your project sponsor is thrilled with the outcome, you could still face criticism if you can't demonstrate that the project was completed in a legal and professional way. Indeed, if you can't show that, you could gain a reputation as somebody who cuts corners, and that would certainly affect senior managers' decisions to use you as a project manager in future.

- *To disseminate information.* Reports are important as a means of communicating information both among members of the project team and those people outside it who need to be kept informed of progress. It can be useful to use standard kinds of formal reports, even where members of the team know informally what's going on. Should a member of the team fall down on the job, he or she won't be able to turn round and claim lack of information. Moreover, managers outside the project team gain a feeling of confidence when they receive regular professional reports which deal with key issues they need to know about. It's a question of creating impressions. If the reports look professional, there's a tendency to think the work is being done professionally. (Which, of course, it is!)

- *To capture knowledge about the project.* Most of the information about how the project was conducted will be in the heads of the team members, but there are good reasons why the most important parts of it should be down on paper. First, should a member of the team leave suddenly – unexpected work transfers can occur, or they could fall ill or under the proverbial bus – it's extremely difficult for somebody new to pick up the task if there's no written information about what's been done so far. Second, if you've completed your project very well – and of course you will! – the paper reports provide a valuable archive that can guide you or others through the same or a similar project, should one arise.

- *To meet statutory obligations.* Some projects – especially those involving construction – require different reports to be completed to meet the various regulations that govern them. For example, Margaret, who organized the new parish hall project, had to arrange for the completion of reports for planning permission, fire regulations and even entertainment licences during the course of the project, as well as producing regular and detailed reports on the progress of the project for the parish council.

The project file

In compiling relevant reports, it's often extremely useful even in small projects – and essential in larger ones – to keep a 'project file', which is best defined as a central repository of all the project documentation. Depending on the size of your project, this may be a simple manila folder, a filing cabinet or a computer full of information. Its value lies in the fact that there is a central point of reference for all information about the project – somewhere where members of the project can be sure of finding the information they need. It's essential to keep *every* report in the project file, even if team members have their own copies. Indeed, it's important that team members should copy central files rather than remove them – key documents can be lost.

Different kinds of reports

So what kinds of reports might be kept in the project file? A project might need all or some of the following depending on its size and scope.

- *Project statement.* This sets out the objectives of the project and other key information about it (see chapter 1), and is a key reference document for all members of the team.

- *Project plans.* These are documents drawn up by individual team members which set out their own responsibilities and how they plan to achieve them. In a sense, team members' project plans are like mini project statements describing their part of the project.

- *Minutes of meetings.* All meetings which the project team holds should be minuted. The minutes don't need to be lengthy – in fact, they're better minutes when kept short – but they must be comprehensive, and they must accurately record every decision together with details of who is responsible for carrying it out. Minutes ensure there is no confusion about what decisions were taken, and that no decisions get overlooked. It's also sometimes useful if meetings between individual members of the team – as opposed to the whole team – are minuted. There's probably no need to do this for informal discussions, but if a handful of members are sitting down to hold a discussion on an important point, there's value in minuting that for the same reasons as whole-team meetings.

- *Budgets and expenditure*. The project budget must exist as a formal document. Expenditure against budget should also be regularly recorded. Depending on the length and size of the project, this ought to be updated every month or possibly even every week. Alongside the whole project budget, team members may need to record budgetary and expenditure information about their portion of the project.

- *Contracts and estimates*. It's vitally important that the project file holds a copy of all contracts which the project team enters into with third parties. Similarly, where work is being done by a third party on the basis of an estimate or quotation, the project file needs to hold a copy of the relevant document.

- *Acceptance documents and sign-offs*. As a larger project progresses, completed parts of it may be accepted by the project sponsor. Acceptance should be formally recorded and kept on the project file.

The same is true of decisions that have been 'signed off', either by the project leader or by a manager outside the project team.

- *Change requests.* It's by no means unusual for project sponsors to change their minds about what they want during the course of a project. (We'll look at this problem in more detail in chapter 7.) Sometimes changes are comparatively minor. On other occasions, they may require substantial reworking or take the project into completely new areas. No matter how small they are, the project leader should always insist on receiving change requests in writing and respond to them in the same way. All this documentation must be kept on the project file.

- *Progress reports.* Finally, the project team may provide progress reports to the project sponsor or others, or even for regular meetings of the team. Again, they need to be kept on file.

As you can see from this list, you could need to provide a wide range of reports and while many of these will be short, some could be sizeable documents. Remember that other people will see your project, and the progress it's making, through the reports. It's vital, therefore, that you shouldn't skimp on the quality of the reports, especially where they're being reviewed by people outside the project team. Writing good reports is dealt with in detail in *The Perfect Report*, another title in this series. You may also find *Perfect Business Writing* of value.

CHAPTER 6

Working together

THE PERFECT TEAM

How does a group of disparate people all with their own quirks and foibles become the perfect team? It is not an easy task welding a group of people, many of whom may not have met before, into a cohesive team working harmoniously towards a common objective. Yet, as project manager, it is one of the most important tasks you have to perform. At the end of the day, the success of the project will depend not just on your own efforts, but on the collective contribution of the whole team.

A good starting point is to recognize that as a team comes together, it goes through three distinct phases:

- getting together
- coming together
- working together

As leader you should be aware that team members will react to one another in both positive and negative ways during each of these phases. Your task as project manager is to shape the way each of these phases takes place so that you accentuate the positive and develop a creative working group, the perfect team. Let's look at the key issues in each of these phases.

Getting together

This is the phase immediately following your choice of members of your project team. Everybody is new and perhaps apprehensive about their role in the project. Possibly, team members may know one another. On the other hand, you may have recruited a team of complete strangers. Or, most members may know one another, but there are one or two outsiders. Whichever of these situations you are in, you have a job to do in order to ensure that every member of the team gets to know one another. Even where people already seemingly know one another, there may be areas of tension between some team members which you need to address right at the outset.

It's often a good idea to have a team-forming event of some kind. Just how elaborate this event is depends on the size of the project team. It could be nothing more than an informal get together over tea and biscuits or, possibly, an introductory lunch. In larger projects, team members sometimes hold 'bonding' weekends in country hotels, but it's unlikely that in a small to medium-sized project your budget would run to that sort of activity. The main point is to gather team members together in a social rather than a working environment, so they can concentrate on relating to one another without the additional pressure of focusing on a specific work agenda. That's not to say people won't discuss the project informally. Indeed, talking about it is often a good ice-breaker when people haven't previously met.

As project manager you should be the key facilitator of this event – not exactly the life and soul of the party, but certainly ensuring that everybody is properly introduced to everybody else. You should also try to take a step back and look at what's happening in the group. Are relationships bonding effectively? Are there potential tensions between any individuals? Does anybody look like being left out? Who's going to be the forceful one? Who's going to be the shy one? After the event, you should have formed a good preliminary idea about the characters and personalities of your team members.

Coming together

At first glance, getting together and coming together might seem similar. In fact, there's a key difference. The first phase is all about meeting other members of the team. This second phase is about learning how to work with other members of the team. Where people have not worked with one another before, there will be a learning phase as everybody tries to come to terms with the different working methods in the group. People will be sizing up their own skills against those of other team members. They'll be assessing what their contribution will be in relation to others. They'll be forming judgements about the skills and abilities of their colleagues, and relationships will be forming between members of the team.

As project manager, you have an important task to ensure this phase of the team formation works smoothly. It is a very dangerous phase. After the first flush of meeting, relationships can go sour quickly if early disagreements or arguments are not speedily defused. In this early phase, all team members will be out to prove their worth. There could be jostling for position within the pecking order of the team. There could be attempts by some members to score points off others, in an attempt to boost their own position. In short, this is the phase of the project when the 'internal politics' of the team can go wrong most easily.

To keep on top of the situation, watch out for signs of early tension among members of the team. Move fast to defuse them, perhaps using the light touch with a little humour initially. Keep an eye open for team members who seem to have difficulty fitting in. Ask them informally about any problems and use your influence as project manager to resolve them. As far as possible, give team members their head – you don't want to constrain the contribution they can make – but try to discourage people from point scoring or outshining others for personal prestige. Make clear that, at the end of the day, it's the team rather than individual contributions that counts.

Working together

It's impossible to set hard and fast rules about how long the coming together phase should last. It will vary from one project to another, depending on the size of the team and the length of the project. However, you should try to move through it as quickly as reasonably possible, without overlooking any of the issues you need to address. Once you reach the working together phase, members of your team should have bonded, should be aware of one another's strengths and weaknesses, should be prepared to value other team members for the contribution they make and should be working co-operatively to achieve the team's objectives.

Even if everything seems to be going well, you still have plenty to do to make sure you're leading a high performance team:

• There will inevitably be disagreements between team

members over issues as the project proceeds. You must resolve those disputes on the merits of the case, while remaining sensitive to different points of view.

- You may find one or more team members struggling with their work. You should act as a mentor to help them tackle their tasks more effectively. (Refer back to pages 59 to 62 for more on this.)

- You must represent the team's work to the project sponsor and others outside the team who may legitimately be interested in its progress. In doing this, you should ensure that you're not manoeuvred into the position of criticizing individual team members for faults or shortcomings. As far as the outside world is concerned, the whole team takes the praise – and the blame.

As project manager, you also help to set the tone as the team learns how to work together. For example, people will take their lead about how to communicate with one another from you. If you're inclined to communicate in a very formal way, the rest of the team will take their cue from that. The same applies to sharing information. If you keep information to yourself, other people will be inclined to do likewise. So be certain that the way *you* are working is the way you would like other members of your team to work.

COMMUNICATING WITHIN THE TEAM

Communication between team members is one of the critical success factors in a project. It saps team morale if members feel they don't have enough information to perform their tasks to the highest standard. Worse, lack of information creates a vacuum which is usually filled with rumour, and rumour wastes time and warps judgements. So, sharing information is vitally important.

Sharing information

How should you share it? The starting point is to make it clear to all members of your team that information is not private property. There is a 'right to know' among all members of the team, unless there are genuinely compelling reasons why some information should be kept confidential. (For example, there might be a case for keeping some personal employment details of team members confidential.) Once again, you set the tone as project manager by making it clear that you're willing to share information.

It's worth setting up some conventions about information sharing among members of your team:

- First, when a team member asks another team member a question, that question should be answered fully and openly. If a team member refuses to provide information to another, there should be an informal right of appeal to the project manager. In general, the project manager should err on the side of providing information rather than not providing it.

- Second, team members should, as a matter of course, provide other members of the team with information which is likely to impact on how they perform their tasks. Information should always be provided as soon as possible and in the most appropriate manner. Often this will be verbally, sometimes written. This not only helps all team members to perform their tasks better, it saves time for the team as a whole because it avoids one member researching information already discovered by another.

- Third, team members should be responsible for ensuring that all the information they provide to other members of the team is accurate and reliable. This is a point that's often overlooked, even by project teams that are keen on sharing information. Where information is not reliable, it's likely to mislead or may lead to faulty decisions. Nothing is likely to inflame tempers in a project team more than somebody shouting: 'I wouldn't have done that if you'd told me that . . .'

Having said all this, there's a final point. While information sharing creates a constructive climate of trust, you don't want it to swamp members of your team in unnecessary paperwork. That means that not every team member has to have every document produced. There needs to be an element of 'information caring' that runs alongside the sharing – the caring being the desire of each team member not to deluge others in irrelevant detail.

Our three project leaders tackled the question of team communication in different ways. In the early stages of her office move project, Suzanne held a weekly team meeting at which members reported on their activities of the previous week. Documents were handed round at the meeting and either looked at there or taken away. As the moving date neared, Suzanne raised the tempo of meetings to two a week. This ensured that even though the amount of information to be shared was increasing, meetings were kept relatively brief.

Members of Tony's project team used electronic mail

to share information among themselves. It was easy to e-mail all members of the group with a couple of clicks of a mouse button, and circulate documents as attachments to the e-mails. This reduced the time it took each team member to circulate information, although it did mean that most team members received rather more information than they needed. There was always a stack of new e-mails to be opened and looked at.

Margaret found that she had to organize communication at three main levels:

- Within her core project team, she held fortnightly meetings which reviewed documents from third-party suppliers, as well as reports from other members of the team.
- Relevant team members held meetings with the main contractors.
- There was also the task of reporting to the monthly meeting of the members of the parish council, only some of whom were on the project team.

Margaret found this triple-level communication took a significant amount of time, but admitted that it was necessary to ensure that nobody could complain that they didn't know what was happening.

HANDLING MEETINGS

Part of the business of communication involves holding meetings – one of the banes of a project manager's life. Meetings are the place where well-thought-out plans can become derailed through a few ill-considered remarks. Meetings eat into working time – not only the hours sitting round the table, but the extra time preparing beforehand and the travelling to and from meetings. So

what can you do to make meetings a productive part of
your project team's work?

Prepare beforehand

Meetings come in all shapes and sizes, from two or three
people gathered round a desk to twenty people in a
conference room. Whatever the size of the meeting, it's
your responsibility as project manager to make sure the
people present have everything they need to hold a
productive meeting. Partly, that means they must have
the necessary space and facilities appropriate to the
meeting. It also means they should be aware of the
purpose of the meeting – the agenda – and should have
all the information, preferably some time before the
meeting, so that they can consider it and take whatever
decisions are necessary.

Conduct the meeting effectively

It will normally be your responsibility as project
manager to conduct the meeting. (Sometimes, you may
delegate this task to another team member if the meeting
is a sub-group of the main project team.) Many people
who work in project teams – whether in the business or
voluntary sector – are not used to meetings and are
nervous about putting their views in them. Your team
members will start to regard meetings as productive
working time – rather than as a waste of time – if you
conduct the meetings effectively.

- *Keep control.* Try to stick to a timetable. Start the
  meeting at an agreed time and finish at a pre-
  arranged time. Work through the agenda systemati-
  cally, allowing all points of view to be heard, but
  discouraging long and waffling contributions. Keep
  the discussion to the point at all times. Make sure

that minority views are fairly ventilated. In particular, ensure that shy and less vocal members of the group have their say – they may be harbouring valuable ideas. Try to steer the meeting towards a generally acceptable decision – but not at the cost of a weak or fudged decision you feel is wrong.

- *Respect the meeting and it will respect you.* That means attending all meetings, unless you have a rock-solid excuse. Arrive on time and don't slope off early – other team members might think you're not pulling your weight. Prepare in advance so that you understand any papers you've been sent. Reading advance papers at the meeting makes you look like a skimpy worker. (These points apply to team members, just as much as project managers.)

- *Put your views and listen to others.* You have just as much right as anybody else to put your view to the meeting. Don't be afraid to speak for fear others will consider you to be speaking out of turn. You're there because of the contribution you can make. At the same time make your points briefly and politely. Don't be afraid to put your view just because you assume other people will disagree with it – you may be surprised by the support you receive. Choose your moment – the right point made at the right time makes more impact than the right point at the wrong time. Listen to other people's point of view. They also have a right to speak. Don't interrupt other speakers while they're still speaking – unless they're talking at unreasonable length.

- *Approach every issue fairly and openly.* You may have clear views on a particular topic, but it's not wise to assume you're right and everybody else is wrong. Listen to opposing points of view carefully. Consider the facts that support them. Test your own arguments critically in your own mind against those put forward by other members of the team. Don't be afraid to change your mind if somebody else has a totally convincing argument. People will respect you for it.

- *Strive to improve the quality of decision-making.* Play your part in finding more information that can help the meeting take more informed decisions. Encourage others to adopt an open and fair stance on decision-making by doing so yourself. Keep the discussion focused on the central issues – 'I think we may be straying from the central point here . . .' – especially if you are chairing the meeting. Ensure the meeting gives enough thought to *how* the decision can be implemented – indeed, in some cases, whether it *can* be implemented – before it's taken.

PULLING TOGETHER

You may have the whole project team pulling together to achieve the same objectives, but that doesn't mean that disagreements won't occur. Indeed, it would probably be unhealthy if disagreements didn't occur – although you want your team to be aiming for the same objectives, you don't want them to be thinking the same way. You want them to think creatively and challenge you and other members of the team with their fresh ideas.

So, in this creative climate disagreements will occur on many issues – although not, we hope, on the fundamentals of the project's objectives. In nineteen cases out of twenty, disagreements are settled after an amicable discussion between the parties concerned. In the other case, the disagreement is more serious. So how should you handle all this?

The first point is that, as project manager, you must set the tone in which every team member respects other team members for the contribution they can make. This is the essential prerequisite for having lively discussions without disagreements degenerating into slanging matches. Every team member has to understand that it's perfectly legitimate to hold a different point of view.

Nevertheless, when a disagreement occurs a decision has to be made. How that's done is largely determined by the rules or conventions of governance that say how the project shall run. For example, you as project manager may have the right to take decisions, or they may be taken by the whole project team. You may need to refer some decisions to people outside the project team, such as the project sponsor.

As project manager, you must make sure you achieve three objectives as you resolve a disagreement.

- First, it must be resolved within the rules laid down for how your project will operate. If there are no rules, you're in some trouble here – probably your word is law. However, if you've read chapter 1 of this book, you should already have a project statement which sets the rules out.

- Second, you must make certain that the disagreeing parties each have a fair opportunity to put their point of view. Apart from anything else, you will only foster resentments if you try to bulldoze the decision one way or the other. You should seek to ensure that, whatever the decision, at the end of the day both parties are prepared to accept it, and are prepared to move forward on the basis of it.

- Third, you must make certain that the decision taken is in the best interests *of the project*. In playing your role as the Great Arbitrator, you must not forget that the main game is not the dispute but the project. You've got to choose the decision which best serves the interests of the project, irrespective of the personalities involved. In some cases, the best decision may be neither of those offered by the two protagonists to the dispute. So don't feel you have to choose between two decisions both of which seem wrong. In fact, you may help to defuse the disagreement by choosing a third way – providing it is the right way.

At the end of the day, a team which pulls together can usually ride most disagreements. And when the team pulls together, that's when you'll find it performing its best work.

CHAPTER 7

Confronting a crisis

FIGHTING MURPHY'S LAW

You've done everything perfectly so far – planned the perfect timetable, recruited the best team, allocated responsibilities, encouraged everybody to work constructively together. What could possibly go wrong?

Well, just about anything, actually.

Murphy's Law – if it can go wrong, it will go wrong – could have been coined for projects. However, the perfect project manager is well aware of the perfidy of Murphy's Law and plans ahead to defeat its worst effects. For the greatest problem with projects is not when something goes wrong – but when it can't be put right – or can't be put right in the time available.

All our three project leaders encountered Murphy's Law as they organized their projects. Suzanne, organizing her public relations company's move to new offices, was horrified to learn eight days before the move that the removals company she'd booked had gone into liquidation. Tony, integrating a new product division into his computer company, found that the data in a key spreadsheet showing forward product sales had corrupted the day before his presentation to the board.

Margaret, organizing the construction of the new parish hall, was told by the builders that they'd encountered an unmarked drain when digging the foundations. Yet none of them regarded these problems as a crisis, and we'll see how they solved them at the end of the chapter.

What generates a sense of crisis is when there appears to be no solution to the problem – or when a series of problems leaves you reeling. You've no sooner solved one before another strikes. You need to expect at least something to go wrong during the course of your project. You should plan the project in such a way that you can deal with unexpected problems as and when they arise.

But how can you plan ahead when you have no idea what's likely to become your biggest snafu?

ANTICIPATING PROBLEMS

The best way to keep problems under control is to look ahead – but if you don't own a crystal ball and you're not blessed with the gift of second sight, how can you do this? When you're setting up your project, there are five key areas where things could – but not necessarily will – go wrong:

1. The project sponsor
2. The timetable
3. The project team
4. Third-party suppliers
5. External factors

Let's consider them one at a time.

1. *The project sponsor*

- *Know what your sponsor wants.* We've already
  mentioned how important it is that the project
  sponsor knows what he or she wants from the
  project, but it's so vital that the outcomes or
  deliverables from the project should be clear that it's
  worth mentioning again. Nothing is likely to cause
  more problems than a gulf of understanding between
  the project sponsor and the project team about what
  the project is trying to achieve. So, as project
  manager, make absolutely certain that you're talking
  the same language as the project sponsor. Understand *why* the sponsor wants to achieve the outcomes he or she has defined, as well as what they are.
  In this way, you'll start to get to the heart of the
  project sponsor's thinking and you'll begin to
  understand his or her motivations. You'll gain an
  insight of those things about which the project
  sponsor feels strongly.

- *Plan for the unforeseen.* That kind of thorough-
  going understanding of the project sponsor will
  remove many of the possible problems that could
  occur during the project, but it won't necessarily
  remove all of them. The fact is that no matter how
  well the project sponsor has defined the outcomes,
  the unexpected may cause them to be revised. It's a
  trait of human nature that people are never satisfied,
  that they see a better way of doing something and
  want to change their minds. So you should plan your
  project on the basis that the sponsor will want to
  make changes as it proceeds.

It may seem like a counsel of despair to plan the project

on the basis of unforeseen changes. In fact, it's more a counsel of reality – and saves many problems when the changes do occur. When planning the project, give some thought to those areas which might be most susceptible to changes. For example, are there any parts of the project where you know the project sponsor was in two minds, or where there was disagreement among a group of project sponsors before the project started? The debate may be continuing and they may change their collective mind again.

It's wise not only to try and identify those areas of the project which may be susceptible to change, but also consider in advance of the project starting how you would handle changes. In other words, will you have a change management process in the project and, if so, what will it be? Obviously, you can't predict in advance precisely what the changes will be, but you can devise an approach to handle them.

- *Formulate a change management process.* It is vital that all changes your project sponsor demands, no matter how small, are handled using a proper change management process. This means each change should be recorded and its impact on the project assessed both in terms of extra cost and time. Before accepting the change, you should report this information to the project sponsor. You must insist that the project sponsor signs-off the change formally on that basis. In that way, responsibility for cost or time over-runs because of changes rests clearly with the project sponsor who initiated them, rather than with the project manager.

Do not be manoeuvred into a corner and agree to accept seemingly minor project changes on an informal basis.

For a start, even minor changes can have an unforeseen domino effect, knocking other parts of the project off schedule. In addition, minor changes have a habit of growing into major changes. Before you know it, you're handling a major restructuring of part of the project without extra cash or time.

Having said that, as a project manager you don't want to appear inflexible to your project sponsor. You want to deliver what he or she wants and you need to display a 'can do' attitude. In this way, you'll be scoring brownie points for the future. By adopting a transparently efficient change management process, you'll look professional to your project sponsor and protect yourself against extra work that's not been planned for.

2. *The timetable*
This is another area where it's wise to anticipate problems. One of the key issues with a project which relies on a series of interlocking activities is that a hold-up in one can have a cumulative ripple effect through the others, multiplying delays. What's really annoying is that it's sometimes something quite minor that causes the hold-up.

When you're drawing up your timetable (see chapter 3) take care to ensure that you don't overlook anything. However, it's tempting to err on the side of caution when deciding how long to leave for a particular action. The problem with that approach is that you end up with an horrendously long delivery schedule for your project which is unacceptable to the sponsor.

- *Rate the risk*. A better approach is to attach a degree of risk to each of the activities in your timetable. Rate each activity as low, medium or high risk, depending on how you judge its chances of over-running or causing other difficulties. Then add in more time for the high-risk activities and – if you consider it prudent – a little extra time for the medium-risk activities. In that way, you've built in the leeway you need where you're most likely to need it, without expanding the project as a whole over an exceptionally long time.

- *Look for key linkages.* In addition, look for the key linkages between different activities in your project. If one activity is not completed on time, what sort of impact will that have, and on what activities? Take care to allow enough time for activities where there are key linkages and pay special attention to making sure that all possible difficulties are anticipated before they occur. The perfect project manager sees problems coming!

3. *The project team*
It may seem strange to suggest that the project team could be a source of problems. After all, its members are supposed to be solving them. However, there are two common sources of problems in project teams:

- *The weak link.* The first is the weak member who finds it difficult to cope with the work he or she has been given. Of course, you've tried to cover this point when you recruited the team, but there's a strong possibility somebody will be less effective than you originally imagined. This can especially be a problem in voluntary projects where people are giving their time free. In chapter 5 we looked at how you can help weaker team members master their tasks more effectively. The important extra point to make here is that you need to identify team member problems and rectify them quickly. If you don't, delays are likely to build up as the weak team member's work falls behind.

- *Disagreement*. The second main problem area is disagreements among team members that turn a relationship sour. We dealt with handling disagreements in chapter 6. In most cases, a skilful project manager will defuse a disagreement and restore effective working relationships. In a few cases, that simply won't be possible. It's a sad fact that there are a few people who, for one reason or another, are simply difficult if not impossible to work with. Many are clever at hiding their quirks, foibles or sheer unpleasantness behind a veneer of sweet reasonableness at interviews. You only realize you've made a dreadful mistake when the project starts and they reveal themselves as a tyrant, a gossip, a backbiter, a *prima donna* or whatever.

  In some cases, you may find that you can manage the individual concerned by warning them about their conduct and keeping them on a tighter management rein. That's never easy, but you might find that you have no alternative. In the worst cases, you may find that you simply have to dispense with their services. If it comes to that, do so quickly, privately and without rancour. Don't get embroiled in a blow by blow account of why you're getting rid of them. Give a simple but honest (well, reasonably!) reason why they have to go. Then make sure they go immediately – on the spot. You don't want them hanging around the office, even for an hour, poisoning the atmosphere.

  Find a new team member as quickly as possible – perhaps there were other contenders when you made your original selection – or redistribute the tasks among other members of the team. You'll find that other team members will generally prefer to take on extra work to be rid of somebody they loathe. You'll also be surprised how quickly the working atmosphere among other members of the team improves.

4. *Third-party suppliers*

Sadly, third-party suppliers are a constant source of problems for project managers. This is true even for experienced project managers who know about the potential problems with third-party suppliers and go to enormous lengths to avoid them. We've dealt with handling third-party suppliers in chapter 4. Here, we need to note that third-party supplier problems tend to be caused by a failure to understand exactly what is wanted – 'I didn't realize you wanted the brochure printed in two colours.' 'I didn't know there was supposed to be underlay under the carpet.' 'I thought all the rooms were supposed to be painted puce.' – It would be only too easy to fill the rest of the book with similar examples. In order to avoid this kind of misunderstanding, take care to specify in writing what you want in precise detail. Don't assume the supplier understands what you mean. Don't be afraid of sounding as though you're treating the supplier like a five-year-old child. Don't deal with anybody who even hints that you don't need to tell them how to do their job. You *do* need to tell them because it's not *their* job. It's *your* job.

Make sure that third-party suppliers confirm receipt of your instructions in writing. Make sure they are quite clear about the delivery date and, what's sometimes overlooked, the delivery place. ('I thought you wanted them at the Birmingham office.') Again, be explicit about these instructions. If you're expecting something to be delivered by ten o'clock, make sure the supplier understands that. If you want the delivery left at 'reception' rather than at 'goods inwards', say so, and make the supplier confirms that he understands.

At the end of the day, most of the third-party supplier problems – and not a few others – come down to a fundamental lack of communication. As project manager it's your responsibility to make sure that communication with suppliers is perfect – and make sure all your team members get the message as well.

One final point: when you find an excellent supplier of any particular goods or service, treat it like a rare diamond. When you are highly satisfied with the goods and services you're receiving, the old adage about green grass and other sides of fences simply isn't true.

5. *External factors*

The final area you need to consider is what we might call 'external factors' – anything about the business, commercial, technological and political environments over which you have no power, but which may still contrive to blow your project off course. In general, there is not much you can do to anticipate *all* the problems you could encounter under the external factors category, but there is something.

Where your project has very strong external dependencies – for example, a research project that depends on the company not being taken over – you can make a judgement about the external dependency upon which the project hinges. How likely is it that the company will be taken over? Have there been strong rumours – or is the likelihood of a suitor appearing extremely remote? Whatever the dependency, look at the factors which determine that dependency, and also what could knock it off course. If those factors look vulnerable, allow for them in your project plan.

CRISIS HANDLING TECHNIQUES

You've taken all the precautions you can, and anticipated as many problems as possible, but, just possibly, you're going to be unlucky. You're going to hit a real-life gold-plated crisis with a capital C. First, let's define a crisis. A crisis is not a problem. A crisis is an event or set of events that, unless corrected, will prevent you delivering your project within any reasonable timescale – or at all. Got that? We're talking meltdown here.

So what should you do if you're in this unlucky position? These six key points should guide you:

1. Assess the full extent of the damage
2. Involve senior management immediately
3. Look for radical solutions
4. Prioritize on what's most important
5. Keep calm but call for more effort
6. Reward people who save the ship

Let's go through them:

1. *Assess the full extent of the damage*
The first step is to know just how bad the crisis is. What damage is it going to do to the project? Don't try to minimize the problem – be brutally realistic. If you underplay the gravity of the position, you will not be able to mobilize the resources or the effort to deal with it.

2. *Involve senior management immediately*
Don't allow the crisis to drift along, hoping you'll somehow be able to get it to come right. If there's a real

problem, get your project sponsor involved straight away, and be completely open about the full extent of the crisis. Most crises occur as the result of those hard-to-pin-down external factors we mentioned in the previous section, so it's unlikely to be your fault. If senior management want to rescue the project they'll make available the extra resources to do so.

3. *Look for radical solutions*
Crises call for radical new thinking. The crisis might mean that you're not just looking at a change in the rules, but a completely new game. By definition, your present approach is not going to work. You need to stretch your imagination to think of alternative ways. Involve all team members in a brainstorming session. Don't rule out anything as being too ridiculous until you've considered it carefully.

4. *Prioritize on what's most important*
If you can deliver some but not all of the project, look for what's most important. Talk to your project sponsor about this. If he or she could have only half of the outcomes or deliverables, what would they be? Despite the crisis, perhaps you can still deliver those most important deliverables.

5. *Keep calm but call for more effort*
A crisis will test your leadership qualities as project manager to the fullest. Under all circumstances, keep calm. You won't be thinking straight if you don't keep calm. Resist the temptation to rush into decisions until you've talked the crisis through with other members of your team and your project sponsor. Be certain that any decisions you take will be effective. At the same time, don't be afraid to call for extra effort from members of your team.

6. *Reward people who save the ship*

When your joint efforts have saved the project, don't forget to recognize the extra contribution everybody made. In a company, consider paying a bonus or holding a thank-you event such as a dinner. (Invite spouses along if the crisis created a lot of unsocial working hours.) In a voluntary project, try at least to find funds so that everybody can have a small gift. The gesture will reap goodwill out of all proportion to the cost.

PROBLEM BUSTERS

So how did our three project leaders solve the problems they faced?

Suzanne, faced with a removal company in liquidation, first checked with the liquidator whether it would be continuing trading. It wouldn't. That was her low point. She originally invited quotes from three companies. She'd presciently thanked the second- and third-ranked companies for their quotes and had a good relationship with the third-ranked company. They were the most expensive – but any port in a storm. When she explained the problem, they were only too glad to help. *Lesson:* maintain good relationships with other possible suppliers.

Tony found the day before a key presentation to the board that data in a spreadsheet had corrupted. However, as an old computer hand, Tony knew all about data problems. He'd backed up the source data on floppy disks. He went back to the source data and reworked the spreadsheets on a different computer. This involved working late the night before the meeting, but because he had the source data intact, he was able to re-create the spreadsheets.

Lesson: always back up important data – and keep the back-up disks in a safe place.

Margaret was told by the parish hall builders they'd encountered an unmarked drain under the new parish hall site. However, Margaret had been briefed by the builders that foundations could cause unexpected problems in building projects. Given the nature of the site, she'd marked foundation building as a high-risk activity in her plan. So, there was extra time to deal with it.

Lesson: anticipate possible high-risk problems when drawing up your project plan.

CHAPTER EIGHT

Bringing it home

THE HOME STRAIGHT

There's a week before your project is due to be delivered. Everything seems to be going fine. You're on schedule and the remaining pieces are ready to fall into place. You can start to think of breathing a sigh of relief. Or can you?

Well, not quite. The fact is that until the project is completely and satisfactorily delivered, as project manager you need to keep on top of the job.

The final checks

You must check with everybody working on the project that there aren't likely to be any last-minute hitches. Beware of vague or evasive statements when you're doing this. If members of your project team are saying things like, 'It'll be all right on the night', or 'I'm not expecting any problems', you should be probing more deeply. These kinds of statements suggest there are problems which still need to be resolved.

In fact, the way to make a thorough check with your team is to ask them *why* they're confident that their part of the project will be delivered satisfactorily on time.

94

They should be able to explain clearly and concisely how all the elements are in place, or will definitely be in place. If they can't, you just identified a problem you didn't know you had.

You also have other responsibilities as project leader. With the project close to delivery, you need to make a final check to ensure that you've met every point in the project statement. Be completely certain that what you're about to deliver is exactly what the project sponsor wants. If you find any discrepancies, take action to deal with them immediately. Don't try to fudge the issue and hope the project sponsor won't notice.

One of the irritating problems with projects is that it's often some comparatively minor detail that lets the project down. Take Margaret's parish hall project. The new hall was successfully built but, just two days from the official opening, Margaret realized the rose bushes for the formal garden round the repositioned war memorial hadn't been planted. She spotted it on time and took action, but others with less attention to detail might miss such a small item after such a long and exhausting project.

The handover

As the project nears completion, you need to prepare for the formal handover to the sponsor. There comes a time when you have to say: 'This is what you asked us to do, and here it is.' Whether the handover takes place formally – as in the case of the parish hall – or whether it's informal depends on the nature of the project. If, like Tony's new business division integration project, you're organizing something which doesn't actually have physical substance, there's nothing concrete to hand over. Even so, there's no reason why you shouldn't meet with your sponsor and informally declare the project complete.

As you hand over the project, don't forget to include all the members of your team in any glory that's going. Nothing leaves such a sour taste in people's mouths as a project leader who hogs all the kudos. You may feel the project is over and it doesn't matter, but if you're asked to take charge of a new project, the others will remember, and your reputation may also have travelled around a grapevine to precede you when you try to recruit your new project members.

DELIVERING ONE HUNDRED AND TEN PER CENT

We've mentioned above that you must check that you are delivering exactly what your project sponsor wants. If you do that you'll have a satisfied sponsor, but, let's be blunt, the world is full of people who deliver satisfactory performance and never get anywhere. What can you do to make your project that extra bit special? How can you turn a satisfied sponsor into a delighted sponsor?

- The first point is subtle but, nevertheless, important. It's perfectly possible to deliver precisely what the sponsor asked for and still not quite meet his or her expectations. That's because no matter how carefully you define the project, there's always that last little bit that the sponsor hasn't told you. Perhaps it's something that the sponsor can't quite articulate, or won't articulate because it seems to be asking for too much. The most perfect project managers have a kind of sixth sense which recognizes this and enables them to get inside the sponsor's head to understand those unspoken aims and wants.

- In many cases, this extra element comes down not so much to what's going to be done, but how it's done and presented at the end of the day. Will the project be presented in a style which delights the sponsor – or will style or manner of presentation jar slightly? It's this kind of issue that often makes the difference between satisfaction and delight.

- The next point you should ask yourself is whether there's anything extra you could deliver that the sponsor didn't ask for, but which would add that 'finishing touch'. Obviously, we're not talking about a major departure from the project specification involving a substantial amount of unbudgeted work. However, in many projects, there are ways to add extra value without incurring significant extra expenditure.

Take the case of Suzanne who organized the public relations company's move. Her brief was to have the new office open and ready for business by nine o'clock on Monday morning. She achieved that, despite the difficulty with the removal company, but she'd added that bit extra. When people arrived at their new desks, they found she'd already provided a new internal telephone directory – valuable practical help on the first day – and there was a flower in a small vase with a welcome card on each desk. Neither of these cost much or involved a large amount of extra work. It made all the difference to the way people perceived how she'd completed the project. In many projects, there are opportunities to add these final touches.

- Finally, don't imagine that just because you've handed over the project and it's been accepted, the project is over. There may be all manner of tidying-up activities before you can finally stamp a closed sticker on the front of your project file. For example, there may be suppliers to pay, maintenance contracts to organize, snagging details to resolve. All these may seem tedious after the climax of project acceptance but they are a necessary part of completing the job you've been given.

LEARNING FROM THE EXPERIENCE

Managing a project should be a learning experience for you. Taking part in the project should be a learning experience for members of your project team. You can learn from one another and complete the project as more rounded managers than you started.

What and how can you learn from a project?

- Let's look at the 'what' first. Depending on the nature of your project, you could learn key new skills in the three main areas that we identified in chapter 2 – functional, management and inter-personal. Flip back to the section 'Identifying skills' on page 14 and refresh your memory. At the outset of the project, you'll probably recognize those areas where you're already knowledgeable and experienced and those where you'll be embarking on something new. In the hurly-burly of the project, there is always a temptation to push ahead, just to get the work done on time, but it pays if you can organize the project to give you – and members of your team – time to learn as you progress.

- One way to do this is to try and take time out at the

end of the week to review what's happened. If you have a full-time project team, consider setting aside the last hour or so on Friday afternoon for a reasonably relaxed overview of what's been achieved during the week. Use this session not only to review progress but to consider ways in which team members have been learning. Encourage team members to talk openly about the problems they've encountered during the week, and the approaches they've used to solve them.

- Next, make sure you document key project information as you go along. There's always a temptation to keep information in your head, rather than going to the trouble of writing it down and keeping it in the project file. However, apart from the fact that written-down information is more accessible to other team members, it also makes it easier to learn from. The very act of writing down something focuses your mind on the key issues and forces you to structure them in a logical way – and the fact that it is written down means you and other people can refer back to it whenever you need. In other words, your written archive should become a valuable source of information about how to organize similar projects.

- Finally, your project may put you in touch with all kinds of useful contacts. These include the project sponsor and his or her associates, members of your project team, other people within the organization for which you conducted the project, and third-party suppliers. Whether yours is a business or a volunteer project, contacts are always valuable. Make sure you record them and keep them – if your project is a success, you could find yourself needing them again.

PERSONAL DEVELOPMENT

The project file is closed. You've left the office and locked the door behind you. The project is over, but the benefits you've gained are only just starting. If you're the kind of person who likes a challenge, you should have gained enormously from the project – and not just in terms of the kind of formal work experience that looks good on a CV – although that's certainly not to be under-rated.

If the project was a *real* challenge – and those are ultimately the most satisfying – you should have found out at least something new about yourself. Perhaps you've discovered some ability or talent you didn't realize you had. Perhaps you've uncovered some new skill that can now be put to use in other projects or activities.

Have a rest. Recover from your efforts – but don't take too long. Projects are like buses. There will be another one along in a little while.